Welcome to...

Our House For Tea

For R, B, E - I love you once, I love you twice, I love you chicken noodle soup and rice

Contents

Introductions

Everyday Easy

Contents

Making An Effort

Contents

Sweet Stuff and Nonsense

Contents

Low-FODMAP Lifehacks

All About Me – What DO You Eat?

Maybe you have just started on the low-FODMAP diet, maybe you have just been diagnosed with Coeliac disease, maybe you have found out the mysterious stomach cramps are down to an intolerance to a particular food, maybe you have a friend or family member with specific dietary needs that you need to cater for: all these come down to the same question – What on earth CAN you eat?!

This book is full of recipes and suggestions for all occasions, there's no need to feel like the awkward eater at a table, the tricky guest that makes people's heart sink, when you tell them what you can't eat. This is food for everyone, 'normal' and 'freaky' eaters alike.

For as long as I can remember, I have been plagued by the symptoms of IBS (Irritable Bowel Syndrome). My mum was fairly sure it was down to something I was eating but as our diet was unprocessed, homegrown and full of wholesome nutritious things, it was difficult to know what.

By the time I left university my face was slowly disappearing into my neck making my eyes look tiny, my stomach was barrel-shaped. I was constantly constipated and miserable. I met my husband, had two gorgeous babies and found myself looking at a pair of size 22-24 (UK size) knickers. Something had to give, something other than my knicker elastic.

I started trying to eliminate foods, starting with wheat, as I had done previously. This worked a little. I had noticed that my hangover when I drank wine or beer, was disproportionate to the units I'd consumed. This led me to cutting out yeast or anything fermented. Every time I had previously seen a doctor about constipation I was told to eat more fibre. I noticed that actually very high-fibre caused an immediate reaction, as did cow's milk. This all helped my investigations.

I became aware of more things that were triggering nausea, stomach cramps, constipation, bloating and generally feeling ill, so I eliminated all these together and I started shrinking. It was very easy to start wearing size 16 clothes but there were still foods I couldn't put my finger on. Why, after only a small apple snack, did I have such stomachache? Was I getting enough nutrients while I was cutting everything out?

I plucked up the courage to return to the doctor almost certain of the reception that I'd get. However, it was a new doctor and, bless her heart,

All About Me – What DO You Eat?

she referred me to a dietician to check that what I was doing was healthy. Having been given the brush off by the medical profession for many years I was expecting to hear the hymn of the high fibre diet.

All About Me – What DO You Eat?

As I explained the seemingly random collection of foodstuffs to the dietician, he started asking odd questions, how was I with onions? Did I drink milk? Then he explained about a trial that was underway at King's College of the peculiarly named low-FODMAP diet, a management for the symptoms of IBS. I had found my kryptonite - Fermentable Carbohydrates. The problem I had, actually existed, it had a name. The relief was such that I could have kissed him.

The diet seemed incredibly tricky to get my head around but I did it. After 4 days my husband leveled a compliment at me that I had never heard before - "Your stomach's really flat". The bloated-ness dissipated, the constipation went, and I waved a happy farewell to the stomach cramps, nausea and headaches. I dropped to a size 12(UK) but interestingly, I only lost a few kilos. I'm still only 4-5 kilos lighter than I was in the dark, miserable pre-low-FODMAP days.

I noticed a similar pattern in my daughter's constitution and after discussing it with the dietician she joined the low-FODMAP diet trial. Success! Her bloating, stomach pain and constipation disappeared and she is a happier, healthier little girl who knows the diet inside out. Interestingly, she is happy to avoid high-FODMAPs through choice, as she doesn't want to go through all the painful side effects.

My son and husband have cast iron constitutions and it's important for me that we eat together at teatime. I don't like hundreds of separate dishes for everybody, so it was equally important that I developed recipes that we could all enjoy together.

I am not a trained dietician, doctor or nutritionist but I consider myself qualified to share with you my vast experience of coping with the constraints of a very restricted diet in a busy life - I love food and I'm not prepared to miss out on the pleasure of eating good food.

Whilst it is easy enough to cater for the 4 of us, it is easy to miss out of my favourite bit of eating – eating with other people. It's good for the soul to share a meal. I've developed this book in the hope that you will be able to share enjoyable meals with family and friends, socialising around food again. Next time someone asks "What DO you eat?" you can show this book – "Come to our house for tea and we'll eat this!"

What is The Low-FODMAP Diet?

The Low-FODMAP diet was developed by researchers at Monash University, Australia, for the management of IBS (Irritable Bowel Syndrome) symptoms.

FODMAP stands for Fermentable Oligosaccharides, Disaccharides, Monosaccharides and Polyols – these are a collection of carbohydrates that are poorly absorbed in the small intestine and broken down (fermented) by bacteria in the large intestine.

For IBS sufferers, these carbohydrates can cause a range of symptoms: bloating, diarrhea, constipation, nausea and stomach cramps, that can often be improved by a Low-FODMAP diet. Living with these symptoms can cause distress and upset; I felt constantly ill.

King's College research indicates about 70% of people living with IBS see an improvement in their symptoms following the diet.

Low-FODMAP does not necessarily mean no-FODMAPs - after the initial elimination period, foods are re-introduced to see which foods you are able to tolerate. In my case, everything I have re-introduced has caused a bad reaction.

The Low-FODMAP diet can mean life without IBS-controlling medications and their side effects, and can free up GP time for other matters. Everyone's a winner!

My Low-FODMAP Survival Guide

Hungry? Just pop into any eatery and get whatever you fancy.

My mistake, we can't. If you are hungry it is very difficult to make the right choices and you invariably end up eating something that you shouldn't and ruining your day.

Life on a restricted diet requires planning. Initially the thought of planning every meal and snack can be entirely overwhelming and off-putting but do believe me, it gets easier. I now slip something from the freezer into my handbag, as naturally as picking up my keys.

In addition to the general melee of family life, cooking from scratch, to prevent my daughter and me becoming ill, can be difficult - I do have a life to be getting on with.

Here are some tips to stop you going low-FODMAP crazy:

Make friends with your local butchers/ fishmongers. Our butcher makes us special low-FODMAP sausages. I buy an entire batch, bagged in pairs for quick defrosting, to keep in the freezer. Some sausages go to the school kitchen for the Little Miss's dinners. The sausages also make impromptu meatballs or stuffings.

If you are catering for a child, don't be afraid to ask what food will be at a birthday party. Actually, that goes for adults too. You can offer to make something that will look similar. I think the offer of help can be a massive relief for the host. As much as they may love to be with you (!) they will have more important party planning to do than making a meal for one.

Packed lunches often fail when you're starving hungry at 3pm, having eaten all your lunch soon after arriving. Make sure you have enough food to realistically see you through the day. Leaving later than planned and stopping at a corner shop for a pasty on the way home is not an option. So in the manner of any Scout or Guide, be prepared; never leave the house without some suitable, emergency food in your bag.

On this theme, it is a difficult diet to get your head around. Most people understand what dairy-free, vegetarian or gluten-free may be – they cannot be expected to understand the vagaries of FODMAP's. Be tolerant of questions. Particularly the 'what DO you eat?' question.

If you are planning to go out for a meal, try and see a menu beforehand.

My Low-FODMAP Survival Guide

There probably isn't anything you can eat on it but is there anything you think could be adapted? Call ahead, (be polite, they're under no obligation to feed you!) ask if you can have things taken off, clarify ingredients, suggest substitutions. The chefs would rather feed you food to make you happy and have your custom, than have you stay away. I really feel this needs to be done BEFORE you are sitting at the table. It is a lot of pressure to put on the waiting staff and kitchen if you suddenly start making complicated demands. Your dining companions will also breathe a sigh of relief, if you don't have to go into a lengthy dissection of the menu at the table. Otherwise, eat before you go out, have a light salad (no dressing) and get a bag of chips on the way home.

Similarly, if you are going to stay somewhere, call before hand. Two hotels I have stayed in have been absolutely marvelous in their preparation and care for the Little Miss and me. I had had lengthy emails and chats beforehand and it really meant that we could relax while we were there.

If in doubt anywhere, offer to self-cater. Not ideal but given the choice of bringing our own milk and cereal or being constantly hungry and ruin the time away for everyone else, I know which I'd prefer. Some places and people will never be able to see beyond 'faddy eater', let them get on with it*. They will miss out on your sparkling company and custom, while you will be busy being fabulous elsewhere.

*See also the opinionated questioners - "Why don't they have these so-called gluten-free problems in third world countries? Why have all these so-called problems started now? When I was younger, we ate everything and no-one was ill." Well random stranger, whose opinion I didn't ask for, I don't know. But I do know it is very real for my daughter and me, here and now.

Guide to Ingredients

All these recipes are low-FODMAP but most are also free from eggs and yeast. I also have a cow's milk intolerance so all the dairy I use is either from goats, sheep or buffalo. By all means use cow's milk butter and hard cheese if you are able.

I use the Monash University guidelines for portion sizes and cannot stress how useful the Monash University Low-FODMAP app is. For example, although I cannot tolerate a full 250ml portion of orange juice, the app tells me most individuals with IBS can tolerate a 125ml portion. Though there will be individual exceptions, it is an excellent resource to have to hand.

Specialist foods for restricted diets are extortionate to say the least. At the time of writing, the gluten-free bread I occasionally buy for my daughter is **8x** the price of the sliced wholemeal loaf I buy for my husband and son. I keep her bread in the freezer to extend its shelf life but it's a handy illustration of just how expensive free-from living can be.

The following suggestions are not prescriptive but I have chosen the most widely available brands.

Goats' milk products have a tendency to taste distinctly 'goaty'. Although a goat flavour can be welcome in the case of a small goats cheese tart, for the most part it can be a rather unpleasant surprise. The only butter and hard cheese I have found to be un-goaty (I really need to find a better word) are St. Helen's products. This creamy butter is actually preferred by my husband to a standard cow's butter. The hard cheese behaves in a way similar to cheddar. Obviously, when you are looking for a goat's cheese flavour, do look for a local producer, you may even get to meet the goats!

Over the years I have with varying levels of success blended my own **gluten-free flours**, however for consistency's sake, I have used Dove's Farm gluten-free blends in this book. The added benefit is that you don't need to build a kitchen extension to store the many half-used bags of various flours that self-blending can create.

Pure Sunflower Margarine has proven to be the most reliable of dairy-free spreads.

If you are not a coconut fan, please don't be put off by the amount of coconut oil, milk, cream and powder in this book – they rarely taste of

Guide to Ingredients

coconut but the fat present in them is the best substitute I have found for dairy when enriching recipes. For recipes that require UHT **coconut milk** (a 'safe' portion is 125ml) I have used Koko Dairy Free Coconut Milk and listed it as 'coconut milk'. Recipes that need canned coconut milk will specify.

Almond milk used to be a problem for us, until I used the unsweetened versions. We currently use the Alpro unsweetened almond milk. It does add a nutty edge to sauces, so I will often blend it with a safe serving of coconut milk.

We use **coconut aminos** as a soy sauce substitute. Although soy sauce is a low-FODMAP ingredient the yeast in it crucifies us. I use Coconut Secret Coconut Aminos – do check the ingredients of any other brands carefully, as many contain onions and garlic. If you can tolerate soy sauce, substitute coconut aminos with a light soy sauce.

You can buy **palm sugar** either in little lumps to grate, granulated form or as a wet paste. As all the recipes with palm sugar involve the sugar being dissolved, it doesn't matter which sort you use. You can also substitute with light muscovado sugar.

Under no circumstances should you replace **canned coconut milk** with a 'light' or 'low-fat' version; it just doesn't work.

Masa harina is gluten-free flour made from hominy – maize that has been through a process of nixtamalization. In layman's terms this is maize that is dried, soaked in lime juice, dried again and ground. I recommend that you **do not** substitute masa harina with any other maize flour. I buy mine online but if you live in a city, you may have better luck in your local shops.

Non-brewed condiment can be found in supermarkets and chip shops. I use it as a yeast-free vinegar replacement but if you can tolerate vinegar, use cider vinegar in the recipes instead.

There are a couple of specialist ingredients, such as No-egg Egg Replacer, but these are ones that I have found in my local indoor market and whole food store – both of which are manned by helpful and knowledgeable staff. What a pleasure it is to talk to them too! Be brave - if you don't know something, just ask. Shopkeepers want your business and you need their goods – it's a win/win situation.

Guide to Equipment

As I cook all our food from scratch, I do use rather a lot of equipment. On the other hand, I am saving us rather a lot of money, so I don't feel too wasteful having a cupboard full of tools!

Digital scales that have a 'tare' setting and can measure weights, water and milk are essential. As are a good set of measuring spoons from 1.5 tablespoon to ⅛ teaspoon gradients.

I use my electric hand whisk a lot. When my last one died, I invested in a super-jazzy one that claimed so many things. It turned out to be a jack-of-all-trades and master of none, I went back to a straightforward cheap whisk and it works perfectly.

Not being one to learn from my mistakes, I replaced my dead handheld immersion blender with one that promised to revolutionise my cookery. It didn't reach the bottom of the bowl properly to even blend a banana, so again I bought a cheap one that is just the ticket.

My food processor was a bit more expensive but I have had it for 15 years and it is still going strong. I have had to replace the lid 3 times, as I smashed it but I could easily find spares online.

Tortilla press – I talk about this later in the book but use it weekly and it is immeasurably useful for making a quick teatime meal.

I will also talk about my slow-cooker in more detail but seriously, food that cooks without effort? Can you really manage to be without one?!

I do have a stand mixer that is useful but not essential.

Finally, the mini-processor is again not essential but once you've used it for small amounts you'll realise that really it takes little room and is terribly easy to clean after small jobs.

Every Day Easy

All the recipes in this book are easy but the ones that follow are the ones that we return to everyday and can be knocked up in half an hour. My day-to-day cooking could well be described as variations on a theme; sometimes the recipes are made with slightly different available ingredients, maybe they've come from the freezer, maybe they've been made in unfamiliar surroundings from an unreliable memory. Don't sweat the details on these recipes – if you need to substitute and have a little more or a less of an ingredient, do so.

I definitely go through phases, sometimes if a meal's gone down well we'll eat variations on the same theme for up to a week – one should never underestimate the joy of teatime without complaints!

If you're catering for a child and they've enjoyed a meal, next time teach them how to make it. OK, you've got me – I'm basically writing this book so that my family can be self-sufficient and look after me and my low-FODMAP foibles in my old age.

Chicken Thighs with Lemon and Thyme

Serves 4

Prep - 5 minutes

Baking - Up to 40 minutes depending on the cut.

8 chicken thighs, bone-in and with skin intact.

2 lemons

Bunch of thyme

3 tbsp olive oil

1 tsp. salt flakes

Freshly ground black pepper.

Pre-heat the oven to 180°C.

We rarely have a proper roast dinner on a Sunday. Sundays from September to May seem to be filled with my rugby playing family either getting muddy or getting un-muddy. All that getting dirty, laundry and boot-cleaning action doesn't leave much time or motivation to prepare anything too taxing. That is when this dish is kicked into play.

I use chicken thighs, as I prefer the darker meat but you can use drumsticks, legs or even breasts if you prefer (although the breasts will dry out quicker). My butcher has lovely big (chicken) thighs and we use two per person. The recipe isn't too prescriptive - cram in a bit more chicken if you need to. Lemon thyme works best for this recipe but it's not essential. The lemons will caramelise – I have a friend who will eat all of these, don't feel obliged to do the same.

Cut each lemon lengthways into 8 wedges. Place the oil in a roasting tin with the thyme. Turn the chicken over in the oil until the thyme is evenly scattered between the chicken pieces. Wedge the lemon pieces between the chicken pieces and sprinkle over the salt before grinding black pepper liberally over the top of each thigh.

Bake for 35-40 minutes if using thighs, 15 minutes if using breasts. Put a sharp knife through the thickest part of the joint to check the juices run clear before serving.

Served with mashed potatoes, jacket potatoes or anything else that can soak up the lovely pan juices. These lovely herby-lemony morsels can also be served cold as part of a picnic.

Chilli and Courgette Spaghetti with Crab or Prawns

Serves 4

Prep - 15 minutes

320g gluten free dried spaghetti

½ tsp. salt

2 tbsp. garlic oil

50g butter

1 small red chilli, deseeded and finely chopped

2 medium courgettes

325g cooked prawns or 300g cooked crabmeat.

Large handful of flat leaf or curly parsley

Salt and freshly ground pepper for seasoning.

Gosh, this is an easy recipe – I feel a bit of a fraud telling you how to make it. Everyone in our house loves prawns and a bag of frozen prawns is omnipresent in our freezer. I don't drink wine but if I did I'd be washing this meal down with a chilled glass of cold Chablis. Perfect for collapsing with at the end of a busy week.

Try using a green chilli or coriander with either prawns or crabmeat – there are 4 different meals on the same easy theme.

Boil a very large pan of water and add the salt. Tip in the pasta and cook according to the directions on the packet. Grate the courgettes coarsely and finely chop the parsley.

When the pasta has three minutes of cooking time left, warm the butter and oil in a wide deep pan over a medium heat. When there are two minutes left, add the chilli to the oil and tip the courgette into the pasta cooking water. Stir the chilli to ensure it doesn't catch. With one minute to go remove the pan from the heat then add the prawns or crab into the chilli and oil to heat through.

Reserve a ladleful of water from the pasta and courgettes before draining the water. Tip the drained pasta into the wide pan of prawns or crab, adding the reserved water. Sprinkle over the parsley if using and stir using tongs until everything is thoroughly combined. Season with salt and pepper and serve on warmed plates.

Sausage Bake - That Sausage Thing

Serves 4

Prep - 10-15 minutes

Baking - 1 hour

2 tbsp. olive oil

8 Low-FODMAP sausages (see *Low-FODMAP life-hacks*)

4 tomatoes (around 450g)

100g fresh spinach

4 large floury potatoes (around 900g), peeled

25g butter

Salt and pepper to season

Little extra butter for greasing the lid/ foil

Optional – 1 x tsp. finely chopped fresh mixed herbs – sage, parsley or thyme.

Pre-heat the oven to 200°C.

This dish is always referred to as 'That Sausage Thing' in our house e.g. "I've got some sausages out of the freezer, can you make That Sausage Thing for tea?" If you don't have a processor with a slicing blade then you can slice the potatoes by hand, although it will take a bit longer. I have a scar on my thumb that reminds me why I fear mandolins but if you are braver than I, please use one!

The basic recipe is 2 fat sausages, 1 tomato, a handful of spinach and baking-sized potato per person - you can easily increase or decrease the recipe.

Thinly slice the potatoes. Lightly grease a wide ovenproof dish with the oil. This will stop your slices sticking to the edge. Using kitchen scissors, snip the sausages into the dish in 2cm pieces.

Slice the tomatoes into 5mm slices. Cover the sausage pieces with tomato slices. Scatter over half the optional herbs. Cover the tomatoes with spinach.

Lay the potato slices on top of the spinach in a rough layer and season with salt, pepper and the rest of the herbs. Your next layer can follow a more stylish overlaying pattern. Season the top with salt and pepper and dot with butter.

Cover with a lightly buttered foil top or buttered lid - whatever comes into contact with the potatoes will stick. Bake for 1 hour, removing the lid/foil for the last 10 minutes. The potato top will have a slightly green hue from the spinach – no bad thing, I'm just warning you!

Baked Salt and Pepper Squid

Serves 2-3

Prep - 5 minutes

Baking - 13-15 minutes

300g cleaned squid, sliced into rings

1 heaped tbsp. cornflour

1 tbsp. olive oil

5 long peppercorns, ground with a pestle and mortar

1 tsp. sea salt flakes, lightly crushed

Preheat the oven to 225°C. Line a large baking tray with greaseproof paper.

Gosh my son loves this; loves, loves, loves it. I'd prefer to serve this on a platter but I can't, as it is too difficult to police and be sure that everyone has had a fair portion. Fried calamari rings are delicious but time constraints have led me to this baked version.

I use fragrant long pepper but you can substitute with 1 tsp. freshly ground black pepper. For a hotter version, grind ½ tsp. of Szechwan peppercorns. A very mild version uses 1 tsp. sweet smoked paprika. I use sea salt flakes, sometimes smoked sea salt flakes or my own blend of aromatic salt. If I'm feeling flamboyant, I substitute the pepper entirely with 1 tsp. of za'atar.

In a large bowl, stir together the cornflour, salt and pepper. Add the squid rings and olive oil. Mix everything together thoroughly. The easiest way to do this is using one hand.* When all the squid is evenly coated, spread the rings evenly on the baking tray. Bake for 13-15 minutes until crispy.

Only use one hand so you have a spare clean hand to turn the tap on!

Beef Meatballs

Serves 4 - makes 24 meatballs

Prep - 15-20 minutes

Cooking - 15 minutes

75g Cheese Scone Bread (or your usual gluten-free bread)

⅛ tsp. asafoetida

1 tsp. dried mixed herbs

500g beef mince

Large pinch of salt

Freshly ground black pepper

1 tbsp. sunflower oil

It is imperative you sing 'On Top Of Spaghetti' to start any meatball teatime. Even if you are alone, it is crucial not to miss this stage - Google the lyrics if you need to.

I like my meatballs small, I like them fried before drowning them in sauce and I like to make twice the quantity so that I have a quick teatime waiting in the freezer. Even better, is when I can make the sauce using the Roasted Vegetables from the freezer. Very best of all, is when I can persuade a child to do the meatball rolling for me.

I recommend using my Our Daily Bread in this recipe – not least because of the umami element it brings to the balls and the extra texture from the sunflower seeds in the bread. If this sounds a bridge too far, use your regular gluten-free bread.

In a processor, blitz the bread into breadcrumbs then tip into a large bowl. Add the asafoetida, herbs, salt and 5 grinds of black pepper. Mix together with a spoon. Tip the mince into the breadcrumbs and using clean hands squeeze the mixture together until it is thoroughly combined.

Take a piece the size of a walnut and roll together, pressing gently between your palms to create a firm ball. The mix will make 25 balls. Heat the oil in a wide frying pan over a medium heat then gently fry the balls, shaking the pan to turn the balls as they brown. After 15 minutes take a ball and cut open to ensure it is cooked all the way through (if it is, you can eat this one, it is a spare!)

Transfer the balls onto a warmed plate lined with kitchen paper then into your sauce and onto your spaghetti. A smattering of grated cheese on top is crucial for the meatball song to work.

Green Cheese Sauce

Serves 6

Prep and cooking - 20 minutes

80g butter

90g gluten-free plain flour

500ml coconut milk, warmed

200g fresh spinach, cooked and cooled

100g hard goat's cheese, grated

Pinch of salt

Freshly ground black pepper

Small grating of nutmeg

This was invented when my son was going through a Dr. Seuss' 'Green Eggs and Ham' phase. I strewed it all over a plate of ham and poached eggs and although he wasn't entirely convinced that it was technically correct, he was happy enough to eat the results – "I DO like green eggs and ham!"

We resurrected the idea when his sister was being a spinach-refusnik. Needless to say, they are both now wise to the fact that there is no green-cheese and if there were, it would be best not to eat it. That doesn't stop them asking for the sauce on pasta, with chicken, cold ham, as a sauce for fish fingers. Although we have not eaten it in a box or with a fox, we have probably consumed it in as many ways as Sam I Am. A Low-FODMAP 'safe' serving of UHT coconut milk is 125ml. You can use mild or mature goat's cheese, or if you prefer, a cheddar.

In a heavy based pan, melt the butter over a medium heat. Stir in the flour and allow to cook, stirring constantly until the butter and flour come together as a smooth paste. Pour on a little (2-3 tbsp.) warm milk and stir until it is thoroughly absorbed. Add the rest of the milk, 100ml at a time, each time ensuring it is completely absorbed into the sauce before adding more.

Continue stirring until it reaches a thick consistency that will coat the back of a spoon. Add the cheese and remove from the heat. Continue stirring, the cheese will begin to melt in the heat of the sauce. The sauce will still have some small lumps of un-melted cheese. Squeeze the excess water from your spinach, then roughly chop and stir into the sauce to combine.

Using a wand blender, whizz the sauce. It will go from lightly flecked to vibrant green. Add 4-5 gratings of nutmeg, and season with salt and pepper to taste. Warm through again over a medium heat, stirring continually, before serving. I freeze this in individual portions for emergency vitamins.

Rosti

Rosti is an immeasurably useful recipe to have in your low-FODMAP and gluten-free arsenal. It's quick to make and can easily be thrown together if you find yourself at someone else's house for tea.

Officially, you would add onion to the recipe and squeeze the excess water out of the grated potato. Onion is a no-go and a thorough squeeze would involve me asking my hosts for a tea towel, for me to stain with potato juice. I started not getting too hung up on the juice and then wondered why I had ever bothered in the first place.

Baking potatoes and new potatoes produce different results but I think you shouldn't worry, it depends on what you have available. Out of preference, I would plump for a red Désirée. The following method is more of an outline than a serious list of weights and measures.

Heat two tablespoons of fat in a frying pan. For a crispy edge the fat needs to get really hot – I would suggest using groundnut oil, sunflower oil, dripping, bacon fat, or goose fat but olive oil will do if you options are limited.

While the oil heats, grate a large washed potato on a coarse grater, no need to peel, it's a good source of vitamin C. Using your hands, mix in a large pinch of salt flakes and 5 or 6 grinds of black pepper.

To test the temperature of your oil put a strand of potato in the pan. When it bubbles around the edges, it's ready to rock. Tip the potato into the pan and spread in one even layer or 3 smaller flat cakes. Fry for 5 minutes and try not to shuffle it about too much; the rosti needs time to bind together.

When the top is starting to get translucent and you can lift the rosti as one piece using a fry slice, remove from the heat and slide onto a plate. Using sleight of hand, witchcraft or just lots of practice, place the pan back on the heat and flip the rosti into the pan to cook on the other side.

Cook for a further 5 minutes, the rosti is ready when both sides are golden, there is no opaque potato left and it is happy to slide about in the pan without too much breaking up. For a large pizza style rosti, cook on one side, turn over and top with tomato sauce, wilted spinach and ham and cheese. The cheese melts as the other side is cooking.

Baked Feta Cheese

Serves 2

Prep - 5 minutes

Baking - 15 minutes

1 tbsp. olive oil

2 salad tomatoes, sliced

200g block of feta

6-8 sprigs of oregano/ marjoram/thyme

Freshly ground black pepper

Preheat the oven to 200°C

True feta is made from sheep's milk - ideal for our ridiculously restricted diet. If you share our intolerance to cow's milk, it is worth checking the label to see whether it has been adulterated with other milks.

Baked feta falls into my category of barely cooking. Stir the feta into hot pasta or tip onto a pile of peppery salad leaves, allowing them to wilt in the hot juices. You can omit the tomatoes if you wish but I see it as another easy vitamin opportunity. For variety, try using chilli, garlic, basil or lemon oil instead of plain olive oil. Try the suggested varieties of herbs either together or separately. I think I've just suggested 35 different ways of baking your feta – there has to be a combination right for you!

Lay a piece of foil over a shallow baking tin. Pour ½ tbsp. of olive oil onto the centre of the foil and lay on the tomato slices into a rectangle the size of the feta block. Top the tomatoes with half of the herbs then the feta block. Place the last of the herbs on top of the feta, grind over black pepper and drizzle with the last of the olive oil.

Lift the opposite sides of the foil together and fold down before scrunching the ends upwards. Your parcel should now be sealed, bake on the tray for 15 minutes. Take care when opening the parcel as the steam can give you quite a nasty scald.

Chicken Tortilla Strips

Serves 4

Prep - 15-20 minutes

Baking - 20 minutes

400g chicken breast fillets or boneless, skinless chicken thighs

200g gluten-free plain tortilla chips, processed into fine crumbs

3 tbsp. gluten-free plain flour

1.5 tsp. sweet smoked paprika

3 heaped tsp. no-egg substitute

6 tbsp. water

2 tsp. olive oil

Pre-heat the oven to 190°C. Line a baking sheet with greaseproof paper and lightly grease with 1 tsp. of olive oil.

Partly through unashamed snobbishness, I always cringed at recipes that suggested crisps or tortilla chips as a crust. Perhaps I was scarred by the memory of making cricket-ball-sized scotch eggs at school, using crisps instead of breadcrumbs. Necessity forced me to address my prejudice – I needed a yeast-free breadcrumb substitute. I reconsidered tortilla chips; my previous issue was that the crumb was too spikey. However, a really good blitz in a food processor will give you a good crumb that doesn't lacerate the roof of your mouth. Hurray!

If you can tolerate eggs, use 3 beaten eggs instead of the egg substitute and water. I really recommend that you double this recipe and freeze half, unbaked, in a freezer proof container, layered with greaseproof paper. Remove from the freezer to the fridge in the morning and bake as usual at teatime.

Place the chicken breasts one at a time, between two sheets of greaseproof paper or cling film. Using a rolling pin flatten the breasts out until they are around 1.5cm thick. Slice each breast into pieces around 2-3cm wide and 8-10cm long (without getting too hung up on precision!) If you are using thighs, chop each into 4 even sized pieces.

In a large plastic freezer bag (or in a shallow bowl) mix together the paprika, flour and salt. Using a shallow bowl, whisk together the no-egg and water until foamy. Tip the tortilla crumbs onto a plate.

Shake the chicken, a few strips at a time, in the flour mix until lightly coated. Dip the floured strips one at a time into the no-egg (*or egg*) and then into the crumbs. Turn the strips over and press lightly until coated. Lay the strips onto the prepared baking sheet.

Drizzle over the remaining tsp. of olive oil and bake for 20 minutes. Insert a sharp knifepoint into the thickest part of a nugget to check the juices run clear before serving.

Mozzarella Nuggets

Serves 4

Prep - 10-15 minutes

Baking - 10 minutes

2 x 125g mozzarella balls

200g gluten-free plain tortilla chips, processed into fine crumbs

2 tbsp. gluten-free plain flour

1.5 tsp. sweet smoked paprika

2 heaped tsp. no-egg substitute

4 tbsp. water

2 tsp. olive oil

Pre-heat the oven to 175°C.

Oh crikey, this recipe is another insight to our not-too-refined teatimes! Yes, the nuggets are like the ones bought from fast-food. Little Miss and I cannot tolerate cow's milk so we use buffalo mozzarella. These cry out for a tomato-y dipping sauce, which may or may not also have lots of vegetables hidden inside...

I have used egg substitute and water here but if you can tolerate them, use 2 beaten eggs instead.

Cut each ball into 8 even pieces (cut the balls in half horizontally and each half into quarters). Line a baking sheet with greaseproof paper and lightly grease with 1 tsp. of olive oil.

In a large plastic freezer bag (or in a shallow bowl) mix together the paprika, flour and salt. Using a shallow bowl, whisk together the no-egg and water until foamy. Tip the tortilla crumbs onto a plate.

With a delicate touch so as not to break up the pieces, roll the mozzarella in the flour mix. Dip the pieces one at a time into the no-egg *(or egg)* and then into the crumbs, turning the cheese over and pressing lightly until coated. It is important the pieces are completely and securely crumbed.

Drizzle over the remaining tsp. of olive oil and bake for 5-7 minutes. When they are ready the cheese will have begun to leak slightly from the crumbs.

Fish Fingers

Serves 4

Prep 15-20 minutes

Baking 20 minutes

400g fish, dried with kitchen towels

200g gluten-free plain tortilla chips, processed into fine crumbs

3 tbsp. gluten-free plain flour

3 heaped tsp. no-egg substitute

6 tbsp. water

Freshly ground black pepper

2 tsp. olive oil

Pre-heat the oven to 190°C. Line a baking sheet with greaseproof paper and lightly grease with 1 tsp. of olive oil.

I vaguely regret creating this recipe – gluten-free, dairy-free, egg-free, yeast-free fish fingers are one of the very few 'processed' foods we can buy and now the children are no longer content with the shop bought ones. Basically, it's the same recipe as the chicken strips, still celebrating the versatility of a super-crushed tortilla chip.

You will need a firm fish such as haddock, salmon, pollock, hake or cod - these are much easier to cut into regular shapes. I have used egg substitute and water here but if you can tolerate them, use 3 beaten eggs instead.

Using a large sharp knife cut the fish into 1.5 cm evenly sized rectangles, or at least as evenly as you can manage.

Place the tortilla crumbs on a large plate. Put the flour into a large plastic freezer bag and season with the salt and pepper. Taking 4 pieces at a time, gently toss the fish in the flour until it is coated on all sides.

Whisk together the egg replacer and water until foamy. Dip the fish into the no-egg mix *(or egg)* and onto the plate of tortilla crumbs. Cover with the crumbs and press down until it is evenly coated. Place onto the baking sheet and repeat until all the pieces are used up. Drizzle with the last of the olive oil and bake for 15 minutes.

Chicken-I-Love

1 portion

Prep - 10-15 minutes

Baking - 20 minutes

Large chicken breast

2 fresh sage leaves

1 slice Serrano or Parma ham

70g gluten-free plain tortilla chips, processed into fine crumbs

1 ½ tbsp. gluten-free plain flour

1 heaped tsp. egg replacer

2 tbsp. water

1 tsp. olive oil

Salt and freshly ground black pepper

Pre-heat the oven to 190°C/ 175°C (fan)/ gas mark 5. Line a baking sheet with greaseproof paper and lightly grease with ½ tsp. of olive oil.

The unusual name for this dish comes courtesy of The Little Miss – a sort of schnitzel with elements of saltimbocca, via KFC. Classy.

This recipe is for one portion to allow you to scale up easily as needed. If you can tolerate eggs simply use 1 beaten egg instead of the egg substitute and water.

Place the chicken between two sheets of greaseproof paper or cling film. Using a rolling pin and some good thwacks, flatten the breast out evenly until it is no thicker than 1cm.

Place the tortilla crumbs on a large plate. Place the flour on a separate plate and season with the salt and pepper. Lay the sage leaves on top of the chicken breast and the ham on top of the sage. Press down.

Whisk together the egg replacer and water until foamy. Flour the chicken on both sides; dip in the no-egg mix *(or egg)* and then onto the plate of tortilla crumbs. Cover with the crumbs and press down until it is evenly coated. Place onto the baking sheet, drizzle with the last of the olive oil and bake, ham side up, for 20 minutes. Check with a sharp knife-point that the juices run clear before serving.

Nachos

Makes 2 large dishes (to feed 4 as a main meal or 6 friends as a supper)

Prep and cooking - 15 minutes

2 x 200g bags low FODMAP tortilla chips

1 quantity of rich minced beef taco topping *(see Soft Corn Taco Fillings)*

½ cucumber, peeled and diced

2 large tomatoes, diced

200g hard mature goat's cheese or cheddar-type cheese, grated

50g bottled sliced green jalapenos drained (check ingredients for any high FODMAPs in the pickling brine)

200g sheep, goat's or lactose free plain yogurt

Rich minced beef is possibly our favourite taco topping. I use it when I'm throwing any semblance of respectability to the wind and making nachos for tea. The topping would almost certainly have come from a double batch that had been frozen. It's a winner for an evening with friends, who can simultaneously eat with their fingers, catch up on all the news and share a drink or two.

For variation, any of the taco toppings can also be used as nachos toppings. Add a small, fresh chilli chopped into rings instead of the jalapenos, if you would prefer a bit more heat.

Warm two large serving dishes in a low oven. If your beef isn't already hot, warm it in a pan.

After 5 minutes, take the serving dishes from the oven. Place a bag of tortilla chips on each dish, and split the topping over both dishes. Sprinkle the cheese evenly over the top and return to the oven for 5 minutes. Share the vegetables and jalapeno slices over the top of the cheese and blob the yogurt about with abandon. I also like to lift some of my chips up a little, so that you can see a little bit of everything.

Eat with napkins and possibly, a bib.

Spinach and Coconut Curry, with Prawn, Chicken or Beef Variations

Serves 4

Prep - 15-20 minutes

Cooking - 15 minutes

2 tbsp. garlic oil

1 tbsp. coconut oil

Thumb sized piece of root ginger, very finely grated

1 green chilli, very finely sliced

1 lime, zest finely shredded and juiced

1 tsp. ground coriander

¼ tsp. ground white pepper

1 large green pepper, finely sliced lengthways

1 large carrot, sliced into matchsticks

500g cooked shelled prawns

3500ml canned coconut milk

30g creamed coconut

200g baby leaf spinach

Small bunch of coriander, finely chopped.

Back in the day, when babysitting wasn't an issue, my friends and I would often end up in a Thai restaurant in Finsbury Park, incongruously called 'Cats Café des Artistes'. Had I realised just how much of my diet would later become coconut dependent I would have paid more attention to the details of the dishes but I was busy chattering and generally immersed in a 'slightly' booze-fuelled atmosphere. Predictably my clothes would get too tight and I'd need to remove my tights or undo my buttons - thanks garlic!

I've avoided calling this 'Thai Green Curry' as this would be infuriating to the purists (no fish sauce, no shrimp paste, no lemongrass, no palm sugar) but the recipe works for a mild chilli hit that the children can enjoy too. To the relief of my dining companions, I no longer have to adjust my clothing during a meal.

My inauthentic, quick way of making coconut rice is to put 25g of creamed coconut on the top of rice when it is cooking.

In a deep wide pan, heat the oils together over a medium heat. Add the ginger, lime zest and chilli and stir together for a minute. Add the pepper and carrot, stir again, cover and leave for 2 minutes. Stir again, adding the ground coriander and white pepper - the vegetables should have slightly softened.

Tip in the coconut milk, stir through then add the creamed coconut and lime juice. Cover and leave on a low simmer for 15 minutes. Stir in the prawns to combine thoroughly. Add the spinach to the top and cover again to allow the spinach to wilt for 5 minutes.

Remove the lid, stir in the spinach and turn up the heat for a further five minutes. Stir in the coriander and serve with coconut rice.

For **Spinach and Coconut Beef Curry**, use finely sliced red chilli and a red pepper. Substitute prawns for 500g beef frying steak cut into ribbons – this should be thoroughly browned off before adding the coconut milk. I find this version benefits from a teaspoon of palm sugar added with the creamed coconut.

Substituting the prawns for 500g of chicken strips can make **Spinach and Coconut Chicken Curry.** Fry the strips off with the vegetables and continue with the recipe as above.

Walnut Spaghetti

Serves 1

Prep - 15 minutes

75g gluten-free spaghetti

30g walnut halves, lightly crushed

1 tbsp. garlic olive oil

½ tsp. finely grated lemon zest

Small knob of butter

30g pecorino

Freshly ground black pepper

Small handful of flat leaf parsley

Some 20 years ago my brother and sister-in-law gave me a walnut key with a parcel label attached reading 'a key to your walnuts'. I have kept this key through many house moves with the label still in tact. If you have never encountered a walnut key, it looks a bit like a radiator key and allows you to remove near perfect walnut halves. Now and again you will reach walnut nirvana and manage to extract a whole walnut – magic.

This recipe is for one serving, it is a good store-cupboard meal and easy to multiply. I prefer to have walnut halves that I crush with my hands to keep the texture 'random' but you can use straightforward chopped walnuts if that is what you have. Pecorino can be substituted with Parmesan but, aside from the sheep's milk content, I prefer the sharper taste of pecorino. As you will see this recipe mainly involves stirring – tongs work best for stirring spaghetti.

Boil the pasta according to the instructions on the packet.

While the pasta is boiling finely chop the parsley and finely grate the pecorino. When the pasta has two minutes cooking time left, warm the oil in a wide pan over a medium heat and toss in the walnuts to toast. Add the lemon zest and butter to the walnuts and stir until melted. Keep stirring to ensure the walnuts don't catch. Drain the pasta so that there is still a little water left on the pasta.

Tip the drained pasta into the frying pan and stir to combine. Add the parsley, remove from the heat and finally stir in the pecorino with plenty of black pepper.

Aniseed Chicken Wings

Serves 4 hungry people

Prep - 10-15 minutes

Marinating - between 30 minutes - 10hours,

Baking - 40 minutes

2kg chicken wings (around 20 wings)

1 tbsp. olive oil

2 limes

½ lemon

1 heaped tbsp. aniseeds

1 tsp. palm sugar (or light muscovado sugar)

6-7 cm fat piece of root ginger

The French have Pastis, the Italians have Sambuca, and the British have aniseed balls. I love aniseed and was thrilled to realise that aniseeds are available without their hard icing coating. I started to use them with chicken and particularly with chicken wings. It has since become a family favourite not least because it is a chance to eat with fingers. If you can't find aniseeds use fennel seeds for a similar flavour.

Your butcher can remove the wing tips for you with one of their hefty cleavers, otherwise follow the instructions below. Retain the tips in the freezer to thrown in next time you are making stock.

A chicken wing has three parts: the drumette, the wingette and tip. This recipe uses the drumette and wingette. Separate out the parts of the wing by using a sharp, heavy knife and a firm whack through the joint. If you also have tips, set them aside or freeze to make stock.

Peel the ginger by slicing off the outer skin, then slice into thin pieces, similar to the size and shape of a slice of bamboo shoot.

In a large roasting tin, place the oil, ginger, aniseeds, sugar and squeeze in the juice of the limes and lemon. Lightly mix using a small whisk or fork.

Place the chicken into the pan and, using your hands, turn over in the marinade until everything is well coated. Squeeze the meat into an even layer. Cover and leave to marinate for a minimum of 30 minutes, maximum 10 hours in a cold place (below 4.4°C, ideally in a fridge). Pre-heat the oven to 200°C and bake for 40mins, turning the wings over after 20 minutes. Serve with something to wipe sticky fingers clean.

Tortillas and Their Uses

Makes 18

Prep and cooking - 25-30 minutes

200g masa harina

250ml. boiling water

¼ tsp. table salt

I am yet to meet someone who doesn't like a homemade soft corn taco. Naturally gluten-free and low-FODMAP, tortillas are immensely useful. I have made a pile for a party with a mound of pulled pork and salads, for friends to fill to their own preferences. Don't tell the family but tortilla are a useful conduit for all sorts of fillings that are basically leftovers, jazzed-up by a new presentation. You don't need me to do my usual 'this is inauthentic but works for us' spiel do you?

Now for the specifics - if the tortilla is to roll and press correctly, the flour must be masa harina. It was a long time before I bought a tortilla press; I simply rolled the dough between two sheets of cling film. When I finally relented and bought a press, I was surprised at just how quick the process could be – tortilla teatime is perfectly feasible! I have been known to take both the press and my own stock of masa harina away with me for a weekend. So easy, my travelling companions and I made quite the production line, rolling, pressing and frying before eating tacos heaped with soft cheese and fruit.

It may seem a bit extreme to weigh the dough balls as you roll but it makes sense when you want each tortilla to be the same size.

Place the masa harina and salt in a large bowl. Make a well in the centre and pour in the boiling water. Stir together using a wooden spoon, until it becomes like soft clay. Using your hands, bring it together to a ball. It will still be very hot but it will cool surprisingly quickly as you knead. Knead for 5 minutes, bring into a ball and cover with cling film to rest for 5 minutes.

Place a large frying pan or griddle on a medium high heat.

Break off a 23g piece of the dough and roll between your palms into a tight ball: it helps if you press as you are rolling. Press the dough ball in a tortilla press, turn the disc 90 degrees and press again. If you are using a rolling pin, place the dough ball between two sheets of cling film, and turn the dough 90 degrees between each roll to keep the tortilla as near a circle as possible. The disc should between 10-12 cm in diameter.

Put the tortilla to dry fry in the pan while you press the next dough ball. As the tortilla cooks it will become free to move in the pan, after about

Tortillas and Their Uses

2 minutes flip the tortilla and cook until it has little brown spots on both sides. Keep the cooked tortilla warm in a warm dish covered with a clean tea towel or foil. You should be able to get between 4-5 tortillas in the pan at a time.

Ideally you will get some help – one person to weigh and roll the balls, another to press and fry.

You can make these ahead of time by wrapping the pile in foil and putting in a medium oven (150°C) for ten minutes to warm before serving. The steam inside the packet will keep them soft enough to use for tacos.

Tortilla Variations

For a meaty flavor to compliment your taco filling, try using boiling stock in place of water in the dough.

If you would like to try making a **'puffy' taco**, fry the uncooked tortilla in 5cm of groundnut or corn oil, turning over after 45 seconds and frying on the other side. Drain on kitchen paper and top as you would a soft tortilla.

Cut a cooked tortilla into 6 triangles and deep fry to make your own **tortilla chips**.

Our version of **empanadas** are simply a teaspoon of filling in the middle of an uncooked tortilla, that is then folded over and the edges rolled up to seal, rather like a Cornish pasty. To avoid splitting the dough, I would recommend that when pressing the tortilla, you do not turn the dough-disc but leave it a little thicker.

Fry in 3cm of hot corn or groundnut oil for 4 minutes on one side before carefully turning over with a fry slice and frying for a further 2 minutes. They should have started to get dark blotches. Drain well on kitchen towel and keep warm in the oven while you cook the rest.

Soft Corn Taco Fillings

I've dedicated a section to taco fillings but don't feel restricted – these toppings can work equally well as warm sandwich fillings, with rice, jacket potatoes, as part of a buffet. The reason these have gone into the Everyday Easy chapter is because the slow cooked fillings are invariably from a batch I have made ahead and kept in the freezer or a combination of leftovers from a previous meal.

I always put a layer of shredded lettuce on the bottom of my tacos, not least because it's a way of eating another vegetable. I usually have some diced tomato on top too – with very little thought, that's two of your vegetable rainbow sorted. I am faced with consternation at the tea table if the tacos do not have a little grated cheese on top. Generally this will be cheddar for those that can and hard goats cheese for those that can't.

I have not been successful using avocado. The 'safe' ⅛ of an avocado low-FODMAP serving is just too difficult to police, particularly as The Little Miss is littler than me - I equate this to 1/16th of an avocado. This level of food maths is one of my few 'Life's Too Short' boundaries. I'm exhausted just writing the equation.

Finally, a lot of these fillings use grilled, skinned peppers. This is how I skin my peppers -

Pre-heat a grill to high. Chop the bottom and top off the peppers and cut the body of the pepper into 4 lengthways. Remove the seeds, pith and stalk and place the pieces, including the bottom and top, skin side up on a baking tray. Grill for 5-7 minutes until the skin is blackened and blistered. Using tongs, place the pepper pieces into a sealed bag or into a bowl and cover tightly with cling film. When the peppers are cool enough to handle, slip the blistered skins from the flesh.

With the exception of Rich Minced Beef, all filling variations on the following pages serve 4-6, take 15 minutes to prepare and between 20 and 25-minutes to cook.

Soft Corn Taco Fillings

2 tsp. diced dried chipotle

2 small red peppers, grilled, skinned and finely chopped

1 tbsp. garlic oil

500g minced beef

400g tinned chopped tomatoes

200ml water

1 tsp. sweet smoked paprika

½ tsp. salt flakes

¼ tsp. ground cinnamon

¼ tsp. ground allspice

25g dark chocolate, broken into small pieces

Freshly ground black pepper

Rich Minced Beef

In a small bowl soak the chipotle in 2 tablespoons of boiling water.

Warm the oil in a large lidded pan over a medium high heat. Add the beef and brown it off for 5 minutes, breaking up any lumps with a wooden spatula. Stir in the paprika, salt, cinnamon, and allspice then continue to cook for a couple of minutes, until everything is combined.

Tip the tomatoes into the beef, rinse the can with the 200ml water and mix that in too. Add the chipotle with the soaking water then turn down to a low simmer and cover for 45 minutes. Stir occasionally.

After the meat has been cooking for 45 minutes, stir in the chopped peppers and chocolate with a good few grinds of black pepper. Continue to cook on a low simmer, uncovered, for 15 minutes and stir well before serving.

Soft Corn Taco Filings

Chicken, Tomato and Pepper

½ tsp. dried chipotle

1 large red pepper, grilled, skinned and finely chopped

1tbsp. garlic oil

250g cocktail vine tomatoes, each chopped into 8

Juice of ½ lime

Large pinch of salt

300g cooked chicken, chopped

Dice the chipotle and soak in a small bowl with a tablespoon of boiling water. Warm the oil over a medium heat in a wide lidded pan. Stir the tomatoes into the oil before covering and turning down to a low heat. Cook for 10 minutes, stirring occasionally to prevent it sticking. Stir in the chipotle and its soaking water, cook for a further 5 minutes.

Add the peppers, chicken, pepper, salt and lime juice to the tomatoes and stir together until it is all warmed through.

Courgette, Pumpkin Seed and Herb

2 tbsp. extra virgin olive oil

Knife point of asafoetida

1 large green pepper, grilled, skinned and finely chopped

440g courgettes, peeled and diced into 1cm cubes

60g pumpkin seeds

2 tbsp. finely chopped fresh herbs; use a mixture of oregano, thyme, marjoram, or basil.

Warm the oil over a medium heat in a wide lidded pan, add the courgette and asafoetida. Cover and cook for 7-8 minutes stirring occasionally, until browned. In a dry frying pan, toast the seeds over high heat and stir continually, until they begin to pop. Remove from the pan immediately to stop the seeds cooking. Serve the courgette on tortillas and scatter the seeds over the top.

Soft Corn Taco Filings

450g potatoes peeled and sliced into a 1cm dice

3 tbsp. olive oil

A knife-point of asafoetida

Small green pepper cut into a 1cm dice

Large pinch of salt flakes

Freshly ground black pepper

1 tsp. sweet paprika

Juice of ½ lime

80g young soft goats cheese such as Capra Nouveau

Potato, Green Pepper and Goats Cheese

Warm the oil over a medium heat in a wide lidded pan. Add the potatoes and asafoetida, stir together, cover and cook for 10 minutes, stirring occasionally to prevent sticking. Add the green pepper, salt, pepper and paprika and cook covered for a further 15 minutes over a low heat, again stirring occasionally. Remove from the heat, stir in the lime juice and crumble in the cheese.

Soft Corn Taco Filings

250g firm white fish such as pollock

1 tsp. smoked sweet paprika

Large pinch of both salt and freshly ground black pepper

3 tbsp. masa harina

1-2 tbsp. sunflower oil

Very large handful of coriander leaves

½ small green chilli (or whole chilli if you would prefer it hotter)

1 tbsp. mild olive oil

1 tbsp. lime juice

Pinch of caster sugar

Fish with Coriander and Lime

Slice the fish into 2.5cm wide pieces. Mix together the paprika, salt, pepper and masa harina on a plate. Lightly flour the fish pieces in the masa mix.

Warm 1 tbsp. of sunflower oil in a frying pan, and fry the fish pieces for 2 minutes of either side. You need to take care when moving the fish, so that the coating doesn't come away. Do not crowd the pan. If you need to do this in two batches simply warm another tbsp. of sunflower oil for the second batch while you keep the first warm on a plate.

Place the rest of the ingredients in a food processor and blitz until it a lovely verdant green. Taste for seasoning. To serve, place pieces of fish on soft tortillas and drizzle over the dressing.

Soft Corn Taco Filings

400g turkey mince

2 tbsp. garlic oil

2 tsp. ras-el-hanout

Large pinch of salt

400ml passata

Turkey with Ras-el-Hanout

Garlic is not a part of the traditional spice mix ras el hanout but do check your blend before buying. As part of my chaotic attitude towards world cuisine, I find the blend of North African spices works well against a corn tortilla, particularly in the case of empanadas. We like this served with a blob of goat's yogurt atop.

Warm the oil in a wide, lidded pan. Add the turkey mince and brown for 3-4 minutes, stirring and breaking up any lumps. Add the salt and ras-el-hanout then stir for a further minute. Tip in the passata, stir to thoroughly combine and turn down to a low simmer. Cover the pan and cook for 20 minutes, stirring occasionally to prevent sticking, until it has thickened.

Help-yourself Salad Platter

I understand this isn't a recipe as such; it's more of a musing on the realities of life. Some days it is impossible to second-guess everyone's salad preferences and whims for that day. On these days I give up and let them make their own. I don't understand the psychology behind it but I can make everyone eat more raw vegetables by simply putting a few large platters in the middle of the table. They will gorge on seriously large amounts of raw vegetables, which I could only dream of them willingly eating, had I asked them to.

I would serve this with jacket potatoes and a bowl of drained and mashed tinned tuna, with mayonnaise on the side, for those who can eat it and sweet chilli sauce for those that can't. A light dressing of olive oil, lemon juice and seasoning can be served in a jug. Assemble on large platters and see what disappears first.

Suggestions for Your Platter

1 head of round lettuce washed and dried; Topped and tailed radishes, halved horizontally if they are large; Cucumber batons; Red and yellow pepper strips, Halved cherry tomatoes; Hard-boiled eggs; Watercress; Olives; Grated carrot; Little gem lettuce cups; Fennel wedges (Low FODMAP safe serving is 29g); Drained and rinsed capers; Rocket

Peanut Dressing

Serves 1

1 tbsp. peanut butter

Juice of half a lime

1 tbsp. olive oil

Pinch of palm sugar

Large pinch of freshly ground black pepper

Optional - small pinch of dried chilli flakes

A really handy dressing to have – quick, easy and contains a vegetable protein. Pour over rice noodles with some finely chopped, crunchy vegetables or over some steamed vegetables for a quick lunch. I like it with a small, ridged lettuce leaf that can gather up the peanut-y goodness. Multiply the recipe as needed. If you don't have a mini-processor, you mix by hand in a small bowl.

Whizz all the ingredients in a mini-processor or in a bowl with a whisk. Done.

Sweet and Sour Aubergine

Serves 4 as a side dish

Prep and cooking 15-20 minutes

2 tbsp. garlic oil

3 tbsp. non-brewed condiment

2 tbsp. coconut aminos *(or light soy sauce)*

Large pinch of salt *(do not add if you are using soy sauce)*

2 tbsp. light brown soft sugar

½ tsp. chilli flakes *(or more to taste)*

1 large aubergine, cut into 1cm cubes

2 tbsp. groundnut oil

1 large red pepper, sliced into strips

1 tbsp. cornflour

1 tbsp. water

Handful of fresh, roughly chopped coriander

With a limited number of vegetables available to the Low-FODMAP'er, it's easy to get stuck in the same vegetable rut. This recipe is based on a takeaway dish that we ordered some 15 years ago. It was so lovely but unfortunately, we couldn't remember what it was called or even find the menu to know which restaurant it came from. Inauthentic as ever, I cook this in a wide pan as opposed to a wok.

Eat with rice and scattered with smoked seeds as a main for two or as a side dish in a Chinese banquet.

In a small bowl, whisk together the garlic oil, non-brewed condiment, coconut aminos, salt, sugar and chilli flakes to make the sauce.

Warm the groundnut oil in a wide pan over a high heat. Add the aubergine and fry for 3-4 minutes, stirring often, until it has softened and started to brown. Whisk together the cornflour and water. Add the pepper to the aubergine and stir for a further 2 minutes before covering for a final minute. Remove pan from the heat and turn the heat down to low.

Whisk the sauce into the bowl of cornflour and then stir everything into the aubergine. Return the pan to the heat and stir for a further 2 minutes while the sauce thickens. Decant to a warmed dish to serve and scatter over the coriander.

Fennel Gratin

Serves 4 with lots of leftovers.

Prep - 10 minutes

Baking - 20 minutes

3 slender or 2 plump round fennel bulbs

2 tbsp. olive oil

Finely grated zest of 1 small lemon

40g finely grated sheep's pecorino cheese

Freshly ground black pepper, 3-5 grinds

Preheat the oven to 210°C/ 190°C Fan/ Gas mark 6.

It feels slightly delusional to call this a gratin. Roasted fennel with benefits is probably more befitting. Fennel's natural partner is fish but we eat this with all kinds of things. I am particularly partial to the warm fennel and pan juices mingled through gluten-free tagliatelle. You will have leftovers and should use them to top pizzas or toss into some leaves and rename as a salad.

Fennel comes as either a plump round bulb or a long slender bulb. Anecdotally, the plump one is female and the slender one is male: all you need to know is the plump one takes a little more cooking and the slender is the better for eating raw. We rarely have a choice so the recipe bends to whichever bulb you can get. A low-FODMAP 'safe' serving of fennel is 49g - bulbs come in all sizes so weigh to check.

Trim the fennel base and stalks. If there are any particularly brown dinks, slice these off too. Cut the fennel down from stalk to root, through its widest point.

Lay the halves cut-face down and cut into even sized wedges. There is a chance some of these may fall apart but you can put them together again in the dish. Place the olive oil and fennel in a large ovenproof dish. Using your hands, turn the wedge-slices over in the oil ensuring that they are all coated.

Mix together the lemon zest and pecorino, then sprinkle over the fennel in an even layer, grinding black pepper on the top. Bake for 20 minutes until the cheese is golden and crusty, the fennel is soft and any fennel fronds are starting to char.

Carrot and Orange Salad

Serves 6-8

Prep - 10-15 minutes

1kg carrots

3 oranges

2 tbsp. olive oil

Large pinch of salt

3 twists of freshly ground pepper

1 tbsp. lightly ground poppy seeds (optional)

This is a taste of home, one of my Mum's standby dishes as it can be easily halved, doubled, tripled, quadrupled depending on the number of guests that have wandered in. It pleases me that my children now also recognise it as a taste of home - hardly surprising considering how often they see it! It brings colour and sunshine to a dreary day or dreary looking meal. Keep any leftovers for the next day as the salad only improves with age.

If you have a fine shredding disc for your food processor – brilliant, use that. Don't worry if you only have box grater, it will still get the job done.

Peel and grate the carrots into a large serving dish. Cut the peel and pith from the oranges with a sharp knife. The easiest way to do this is to slice off the top and bottom first so that you have a flat surface to stand the orange on when slicing off the rest of the peel. Holding the fruit over the carrots to catch the juice, remove the orange segments with a sharp knife, keeping them as near whole as you can, only slicing in half horizontally once they're free. Let them drop into the carrots.

Add the oil, seasoning and poppy seeds; turn over with a large spoon so as not to break the oranges up. The dish benefits from standing a while and should be served at room temperature.

Maple Parsnip Chips

Serves 4 as a side serving

Prep - 10 minutes

Cooking - 30 minutes

4 medium to large parsnips (approx. 600-800g.)

2 tbsp. olive oil

2 tbsp. maple syrup

Pinch of salt flakes

2 grinds of black pepper

Preheat the oven to 200°C.

Parsnip is such a pretty word and, in our family, often used as a pet name for small children. However, I don't always share the same affection for the actual vegetable. I think this was brought on by a weekly vegetable box scheme that filled the box EVERY WEEK with a good 3 kilos of parsnips from what felt like October to April. My memory has probably skewed the reality of what happened but that level of parsnip overload had a lasting effect.

We eat these parsnips as a chip or potato substitute. I haven't been too prescriptive on the weight or number of parsnips, as they seem to vary wildly in size from one year to another – I suggest one medium to large sized parsnip per person. If you can only get littler parsnips, double the numbers!

Peel the parsnips, halve horizontally and cut each half into wedges – *see illustration for a rough guide to the size.* Cut out and discard any particularly woody cores.

Place the oil in a roasting tin and place in the oven to heat for a minute. Remove the tin and tip in the parsnips – be careful not to splash yourself with hot oil. Turn the parsnips over in the oil until they are coated and return to the oven.

After 20 minutes, remove the parsnips from the oven. Add the maple syrup, salt and pepper, then turn the parsnips over in the tin. Return to the oven for a further 10 minutes.

Cheese Dough Balls in a Variety of Flavours

Makes 28 balls

Prep - 15 minutes

Baking - 13-15 minutes

125g firm goats cheese or cheddar

100g gluten-free plain flour blend

4 tbsp. coconut cream

Preheat the oven to 180°C.

These light little bread-like balls make a wonderful accompaniment to a soup, stew or any other occasion when you used to have a piece of crusty bread as a side order. Served warm with lashings of butter, these cheesy balls smell wonderful and their appearance belies how easy they are to make. You may see a theme emerging here. Try with other firm cheese, such as Red Leicester.

Place the cheese in a food processor and pulse until it resembles crumbs. Add the flour and process again until the mixture is combined and like rough sand. Add the cream and pulse in 10 second bursts. You may need to scrape the sides of the processor. When it is all combined, tip the mixture onto a work surface and bring together into a ball of dough. Roll into 10g balls and place onto a lined baking sheet. Bake for 13-15 minutes before tipping into a tea towel or a warm napkin-lined bowl.

Garlic dough balls

Garlic bread without yeast, gluten, cow's milk and garlic has been one of my toughest challenges so far. My garlic bread used to be a thing of wonder, crusty and soft, so very garlicky and rich. However, my sudden inflating stomach was also a thing of wonder and I'm happy to live without it.

These garlic dough balls are perfect when you want a bit a mindless stodge to gorge on a Friday night – the sort that a delivery pizza used to bring. However they're also delicate enough to split open and fill with a herbed soft cheese or a smear of pesto.

Add ½ tsp. of garlic oil with the coconut cream and bake for 13 minutes – the extra oil will make the ball slightly crispier.

Cheese Dough Balls in a Variety of Flavours

Variety is the Spice of Life

Use the basic cheese dough ball recipe and add one of the following with the flour:

2 tsp. finely chopped fresh curly leaf parsley

2 tsp. finely chopped thyme

2 finely chopped large sage leaves

6 very finely chopped rosemary needles

⅛ tsp. of asafoetida (an onion flavour without the FODMAPs!)

1 tbsp. sesame seeds

½ tsp. fennel seeds

½ tbsp. of poppy seeds.

1 tsp. freshly ground black pepper

½ tsp. sweet smoked paprika

½ tsp. dried chilli flakes

You could also experiment with a teaspoon of dried or mixed herbs.

I could go on...

Smoked Mackerel Pate Two Ways

I have no self-control around smoked mackerel. I can devour a fillet in seconds without accompaniment, ceremony and frankly, a plate. Luckily mackerel is also astonishingly good for you, so I can cross it off my list of things to feel bad about. I have given you two recipes, one for a herbed variety and one with spinach. Aside from being a good way to use up any leftover spinach, the spinach version is a beautiful pea green and doesn't taste too strongly of spinach.

In 10 minutes, this pate will make 3 half-cup servings that will freeze in well-sealed containers for up to 6 weeks - ideal for lunches. Before you begin, remove the skin from the mackerel and any large, visible bones. Smaller bones will be processed and give you extra calcium. If frozen, the pate needs to defrost for at least 3 hours before eating. Eat on gluten free crackers, cheese scones or over the top of a hot jacket potato. It can also be stirred through hot pasta or eaten as a dip.

250g smoked mackerel fillets, skinned

Small handful of flat leaf parsley, reserving 3 leaves

Small handful of dill

100g soft goats cheese

1 tbsp. olive oil

Finely grated zest of ½ un-waxed lemon

1 tbsp. freshly squeezed lemon juice

Freshly ground black pepper

Herbed Smoked Mackerel Pate

Finely chop the herbs by hand, for a coarser texture or in a food processor. Put all of the ingredients, except the 3 reserved parsley leaves into a food processor. Process the ingredients to combine, until either smooth or less if you prefer a chunkier texture. You will have to scrape the mixture down the sides of the processor bowl with a spatula every 20 seconds or so.

Taste for seasoning and add the black pepper to taste. Give the pate a final whizz before spooning either into 3 individual portion-sized serving pots or a pretty dish if serving immediately. Decorate the individual portions with the reserved leaves - just because it's only for you doesn't mean you can't be a bit fancy.

Spinach Smoked Mackerel Pate

100g raw spinach *or* 65g cooked spinach

200g smoked mackerel fillets, skinned

70g soft goats cheese

1 tbsp. lemon juice

1 tbsp. olive oil

Freshly ground black pepper

If you are using raw spinach place in a small lidded pan with 3 tbsp. of water on a high heat for 2 minutes. When wilted, drain well and leave to cool. Squeeze any excess water out of the spinach then put all of the ingredients into a food processor. Process until smooth, this is a pate that is better smooth. You will have to scrape the mixture down the sides of the processor bowl with a spatula every 20 seconds or so.

Taste for seasoning and add the black pepper to taste. Give the pate a final whizz before spooning into either 3 individual portion-sized serving pots or a pretty dish if serving immediately. As for making this version look fancy – I think a final grind of black pepper works well against the green.

Cheesy-Veggie Drop Scones

Makes 24, serves 4-6

Prep and cooking - 25 minutes

290g gluten-free self-raising flour

½ tsp. baking powder

Pinch of table salt

4 tbsp. water

2 heaped tsp. 'No-egg' egg replacer

300ml coconut milk

100g firm cheese (goat's cheese, Cheddar or Red Leicester), grated

100g courgette, grated

Freshly ground black pepper

4 tbsp. sunflower oil

Proving that there are very few things to which I won't add cheese and courgettes, these dainty little discs are snaffled up as quickly as I can make them. The children would like me to point out that they are delicious with ketchup (Little Miss) or HP Sauce (Young Master). I prefer to eat mine with really crispy bacon, tomato salad and an offer from someone else to do the washing up.

If you can tolerate eggs, replace the water and 'No-Egg' with 2 large beaten eggs.

Sift the flour, baking powder and salt into a large bowl and make a well in the centre. Using a balloon whisk, whisk the egg replacer into the water until foamy. Lightly whisk the coconut milk into the egg replacer (or eggs if using), and pour into the well in the flour. Use the whisk to bring everything together into a batter. Add the courgette, cheese and a few grinds of black pepper and then give a final whisk through until everything is combined.

In a heavy based frying pan, heat a tablespoon of oil before dropping in 6 evenly-spaced tablespoons of batter. Cook for 3 minutes one side and turn for a further 2 minutes on the other side. Remove to a warm plate in the oven, heat another tablespoon of oil and repeat until all the batter is used.

Pork Lettuce Cups

Serves 4

Prep - 10-15 minutes

Cooking - 20 minutes

500g pork mince

1 tbsp. sunflower oil

6 cm piece of root ginger, finely grated.

Zest of 1 lime, finely grated

Large pinch of salt

¼ tsp. ground black pepper

½ tsp. dried chilli flakes

200 ml chicken stock

Juice of 1 lime

1 tsp. palm sugar or light brown soft sugar

2 little gem lettuce

½ cucumber, peeled, deseeded and cut into thin strips

1 medium carrot, cut into thin strips

2 medium tomatoes, deseeded and cut into thin strips

50g roasted peanuts, crushed

Handful of basil leaves, shredded

A bit of fun to eat and easily assembled by small, eager fingers, these lettuce cups work well for a summery teatime. In the winter months serve the mince and vegetable strips stirred through hot rice noodles, then top with peanuts. You can substitute the basil for fresh coriander. For this recipe I do not use lean pork mince.

Sometimes I can be bothered to skin the tomatoes, sometimes I can't – I'll let you decide how you feel on the matter. I do all the peeling and cutting of the vegetables while the mince is cooking, laying out the whole lettuce leaves on a large platter. I have tried with iceberg lettuce but I cannot get enough leaves out in one piece. Little gem lettuces are far sturdier when washed and broken into leaves.

Heat the oil in a wide pan over a high heat and add the pork to brown for 5 minutes, breaking up any lumps with a wooden spatula. Add the ginger, lime zest, salt, pepper and chilli, stirring for a further minute until thoroughly combined.

Tip the chicken stock, lime juice and palm sugar into the pork, stir together and turn down to a low simmer for 20 minutes.

Allow the mince to cool slightly before spooning onto the lettuce cups - quantity varies according to the size of the leaf! Top with the cucumber strips, carrots and tomatoes, finishing with the peanuts, basil and, if you feel adventurous, thinly sliced red chilli. Don't expect to eat these elegantly.

Cheese Scones

Makes 13 scones.

Prep - 15 minutes

Baking - 12-15 minutes

180 ml canned coconut milk, plus 1tbsp for glazing

120g hard goats cheese, coarsely grated (you can also use cheddar)

215ml soda water (as sparkling as possible!)

440g gluten-free self-raising flour blend

½ tsp. baking powder

Preheat the oven to 190°C. Line a baking sheet with parchment or silicone liner.

Cheese scones are just marvellous, especially these. When someone visits for lunch, they're terribly touched that you went to the trouble of making scones. What they don't need to know is just how quick and easy these are to make (and that the lovely pan of homemade soup came out of the freezer). We often eat them with soup at teatime or for a weekend lunch with cheese and meats, when we've been out all morning. Please let me assure you that these do not taste of coconut! If you can eat egg, glaze with a little beaten egg.

In a large bowl sift the flour and baking powder together. Stir in the grated cheese reserving 2tbsp. for decoration. Make a well in the flour mix and pour in the coconut milk and soda water. Using a **blunt** knife and working quickly, mix the dry and wet ingredients until they start to come together into slightly sticky dough. Do not be tempted to stir with a spoon or spatula or the mixture will turn into a batter.

Tip the dough out onto a well-floured board then lightly dust the top of the dough and your hands with flour. Gently, but quickly, bring the dough together and lightly press into an even layer about 3cm thick.

Dip the top of a glass or 6cm cutter in flour and cut into scones. Do not be tempted to twist the cutter, as this will affect the rising process. Draw the leftover dough together and repeat shaping and cutting until you have used all the dough. Be warned that the scones cut towards the end won't look quite as pretty as those cut at the beginning! Place snuggled together on the baking sheet. Quickly brush the tops with the extra coconut milk and sprinkle on the reserved cheese.

Bake for 12mins. They should lift easily from the tray and make a slightly hollow sound when you tap the bottoms. If not, pop them in for another couple of minutes but do keep a close eye on them, they turn from cooked to dark brown and rock-hard in seconds. Line a warm plate or dish with a clean tea towel or napkin. Place the scones on top and wrap the edges around the scones to keep them soft and cosy.

Our Daily Bread

Makes 2 small loaves

Prep - 10-15 minutes

Baking - 35-40 minutes

1 batch of **Cheese Scone** dough

Preheat the oven to 200°C.

This has become our default daily bread - finally a yeast-free, gluten-free bread alternative that toasts well, slices easily and doesn't die after a day. I keep mine in an airtight container and it is eaten up by day 4. The cheese element makes for a filling bread so keep the slices thin; the loaf benefits from being sliced with a razor-sharp knife. Toasting a slice will release the most the mouth-watering cheese aromas.

The sharp eyed amongst you will notice this is the cheese scone recipe simply shaped into two rounds and baked - I freeze one and eat the other. More accurately - I double the recipe, freeze 3 and eat the fourth. To freeze, wait until the bread is completely cool, wrap in cling film and then a freezer bag. Make sure you label with the date. It keeps well for a month; defrost fully before slicing. Store the loaf in an airtight container.

Flour a work surface, knead the dough lightly and bring together into two slightly sticky balls. You can glaze with either a little extra coconut cream or sprinkle over a little extra cheese but neither is essential. Place on a lined baking sheet and bake for 35 minutes.

Tap the bottom of the loaves to check that they sound hollow. If they are still making a dull sound, return to the oven for a further 5 minutes. When cooked, leave to cool fully on a wire rack. If you try to slice the loaves while they are still hot, the melted cheese will pull the bread apart.

Our Daily Bread

Variations

The plain cheese version is lovely but I like to mix things up and will find any excuse to sneak even more nutrients into my food.

Matcha is a powder made from finely ground green tea leaves, enjoyed by the Japanese for centuries. The health benefits are supposed to be multiple and many people enjoy the taste of whisked Matcha tea. I can't get on with the flavour as a drink but I do appreciate its umami properties when added to savoury food. Health and flavour benefits aside, what I like most about Matcha is the lovely green hue it adds to an otherwise beige recipe. It's the most wonderful shade of early spring. Simply add 1 tsp. of matcha powder to the flour.

Seeds can either be subtle, such as 1 tbsp. sunflower seeds or a more obvious 1 tbsp. of pumpkin seeds added with the cheese. I find tiny seeds such as poppy or sesame are best added to the top of the loaf before baking.

Herbs either 2 tsp. of fresh, finely chopped or 1 tsp. of dried herbs can be added with the flour to make the loaf match your meal or sandwich filling.

Cheese Scone Tatin

Serves 4

Prep - Depending on your base between 10 minutes and 20 minutes

Baking - 20 minutes

½ mix of cheese scone (use the other half to bake a loaf of *Daily Bread*)

1 portion of roasted vegetables

Now that you've mastered the cheese scone, it's time to jazz it up a little. Savoury tarte tatin is another dish that can be brought to the table to cries of 'Oh you shouldn't have!' Don't tell anyone, but this could be classed as even more deceptively easy than the scones, as you don't have to cut anything out. You can add ½ teaspoon of dried herbs such as thyme, basil or herbes de Provence to the scone.

If you've been paying attention, you will have some ready roasted vegetables in the freezer in a handy approximate 400g portion. If you haven't, I'll forgive you and give you the recipe as well as some other favourite options.

Preheat the oven to 220°C. Grease a 22cm round baking dish (I use an enamel tin) with a little olive oil, paying particular attention to the sides, where it is most likely to stick. Line the base with a circle of lightly greased greaseproof paper.

Tip the roasted vegetables and their juices into the dish in an even layer. Dollop the scone topping on top in as near an even layer as you can; it will look a bit rough.

Bake for 25 minutes, remove from the oven and set aside to cool for 10 minutes. Run a knife around the edge of the dish to loosen the tart. Place a large plate on top of the dish and in one quick move (you may need oven gloves as the dish will still be hot) flip the dish upside down. Give the bottom of the dish a few taps with a wooden spoon to dislodge any stubborn pieces then gently lift the dish off. Carefully peel off the greaseproof paper. For a touch of frou-frou, top with freshly torn basil leaves.

Cheese Scone Tatin

Cooking the Vegetables from Scratch

Chop 1 small red pepper, 1 small yellow pepper, 1 small courgette and 2 tomatoes into inch sized pieces. Toss with 1 tbsp. of olive oil in a baking tin, season with salt and freshly ground pepper. Bake in a preheated oven, at 200°C for 15 minutes. Continue as above.

Yellow Courgette and fennel

If you are lucky enough to find yourself in possession of yellow courgettes use them with fennel to make a sunny tart. You will need 200g of yellow courgettes and ½ a bulb of young fennel, no more than 196g. Trim the vegetables and cut into slices the width of a one-pound coin. Soften in a frying pan with 1 tbsp. of olive oil and a few sprigs of thyme if you have them. When they have started to colour, tip them into a baking dish and continue as above, adding 1 tsp. fresh thyme leaves to the scone base.

Tomato

Slice 4 medium tomatoes in half and fry skin side down in a tbsp. of olive oil until the skins have started to wrinkle. Place the tomatoes cut face down in the bottom of the greased baking dish and pour over the pan juices. If you have some basil leaves, tear these over the top. Continue topping with scone as above.

Chicken Noodle Soup

Serves 4

Prep and cooking - 20 minutes.

1.5 litres chicken stock

1 whole star anise

1 black cardamom pod, lightly crushed

½ tsp. Szechwan peppercorns

2 inch cinnamon stick

½ tsp. fennel seeds

3 cm piece of root ginger, peeled and sliced into discs

200g thin flat rice noodles

1 tbsp. garlic oil

1 large red pepper, sliced in strips

150g spinach

350g cooked chicken breast, shredded

Large bunch of fresh coriander, stalks removed and leaves roughly chopped

1 small red chilli finely chopped

I don't know where to begin with this recipe – it's the culinary equivalent of our North Star. Chicken noodle soup is what we eat when life is busy, when we're poorly, when we're celebrating, when we've got some laid back family time, when it is cold, when the first lot of new vegetables appear in the garden, when I've got some decidedly bendy looking vegetables in the fridge: it is omnipresent and comforting. I don't pretend this is authentic to any particular cuisine – it is ours, it belongs to our house at teatime.

The recipe can be adapted to a degree: take out the spices and replace the coriander with parsley, grate a carrot into the stock as it heats. If you are catering for a lot of people, use all the chicken and light stock from the boiled chicken recipe and triple the other ingredients. We add our fresh chilli at the end to allow for different palates.

Place the stock and spices in a large pan, cover and bring to boiling point. Turn down to a low simmer.

Put the soup bowls somewhere to warm. Cook the noodles according to the instruction on the packet. In a frying pan, warm the oil then stir-fry the red pepper. Stir through the chicken to warm, and then remove from the heat.

Using a slotted spoon, fish out the spices from the stock, cover and return to the boil. Add the spinach and coriander to the stock and remove from the heat. Split the noodles between the 4 warmed bowls. Spoon over the pepper and chicken and finally pour over the stock.

Serve with as much red chilli as you like. Soy sauce doesn't agree with my daughter or me, so while the boys in the family drown their soup in soy sauce, we enjoy coconut aminos and a little squeeze of lime juice.

Carrot and Peanut Soup

Serves 4-6

Prep - 10 minutes

Cooking - 1hr 15 minutes

70g roasted peanuts

1 kg carrots, peeled and sliced

1 tbsp. olive oil

1 litre vegetable stock

Small bunch of fresh parsley very roughly chopped

Salt and pepper to season

4 tsp. of crushed peanuts for decoration

This soup works well when served outside in mugs during a stint of winter garden clearing. Before I came to my senses, I would roast my own redskin peanuts and peel them between two tea towels. You still can roast your own blanched peanuts if you wish but I have found a lazier option – simply rinse the salt off salted roasted peanuts. Don't use dry-roasted peanuts - it would taste horrible.

Once cooled, freeze any leftovers for lunches in portion-sized freezer-safe containers.

In a large pan warm the oil over a medium heat and add the carrots. Sweat the carrots with the lid on, stirring occasionally, for 15 minutes.

Add the peanuts and parsley to the carrots and cover with the stock. Bring up to almost boiling then reduce to a low simmer for an hour. Blend the soup until smooth using either a handheld blender or liquidiser. Season to taste with salt and pepper. If you are using a liquidizer, return the soup to the pan. Stir the pan over a medium heat for a minute or two for a final warm through. Decorate each bowl with a teaspoon of crushed peanuts.

Olive Tapenade

Prep - 10 minutes

250g pitted black olives

20g small capers in brine, drained and rinsed

2 fillets of anchovies (tinned in or jarred in oil)

½ tsp. lemon juice

1 tbsp. garlic olive oil

5 good grinds of freshly ground black pepper

Little extra plain olive oil for drizzling

This stores very well in the fridge for a week, if you keep the top covered with oil. Eat it spread thickly on whatever carbohydrate you're allowed: use it as a dip with crudités or crisps, spoon into a jacket potato, toss into hot pasta or steamed vegetables, top a pizza with it mixed into the base sauce, stir through some steaming new potatoes or spread it on a rosti as an impromptu pizza.

I could go on but I'm sure you have better things to do with your life than read an essay on the uses of olive paste.

The olives and capers don't need to be terrifically fancy, just drain and rinse ones bought in brine.

Either using a small processor or wand hand blender whizz together all the ingredients (except the extra olive oil), until almost but not completely, smooth.

Decant into a sealable container and drizzle a little plain olive oil on top. Keep in the fridge until you are ready for a little smackerel of something salty.

Variations on an Olive Theme

You could add either half a red chilli, 1/4tsp chilli flakes or finely grated zest of ½ lemon to jazz things up a little. Try using green olives instead of black and leave out the anchovies.

Chicken with Grapes and Tarragon

Serves 2

Prep - 10 minutes

Cooking - 30 minutes

2 tbsp. garlic oil

2 x large chicken breasts

4 x slices Parma ham

300g grapes (approximately. 15 grapes per portion)

40g fresh tarragon leaves

400ml rich chicken stock

Salt and pepper for seasoning.

Tarragon, such a lovely, elegant herb but I often over-look it in favour of fennel or aniseed. I have done tarragon a disservice and by way of apology, here is a grown-up recipe. It doesn't really matter whether you use green or red grapes but I would say the red grapes do lose their colour and take on a brown hue. A less elegant accompaniment of mashed potato soaks up the delicious sauce perfectly and ensures you won't need to inelegantly lick the plate.

Wrap each chicken breast in two slices of Parma ham. In a wide lidded pan, warm the oil over a medium high heat then fry the chicken for 30 seconds on each side. Add the tarragon and grapes and cook for a minute, jiggling the pan to roll the grapes. Pour over the stock, cover with the lid and simmer over a low heat for 25 minutes.

Piece the thickest part of the breast with a sharp knifepoint to check the juices run clear and it is cooked. Remove the chicken and grapes to a warmed serving dish and cover with foil. Return the pan to a high heat, stirring often, for 3-6 minutes until the sauce has reduced. Pour the sauce over the chicken and sprinkle with any remaining tarragon leaves you may have.

Jacket Potatoes

Preheat the oven to 200°C.

A spud the size of a 330ml drink can is ideal.

Our family eat a lot of jacket potatoes. If you've only ever encountered the baked jacket potato microwaved with a flaccid, grainy skin, hard, sticky inside and topped with margarine and watery coleslaw, I'll wager that you don't think you like them.

Firstly, pick the right potato. It needs to be floury so choose King Edward, Desiree, Rooster or similar. You can buy enormous potatoes, the size of a guinea pig, specifically marketed as 'jacket potatoes'; in my mind, these are too big to cook properly and a rather overwhelming prospect to eat. The potatoes need to be an even size to eliminate the Russian roulette of 'who gets the hard potato?'

Scrub your potatoes. Although the heat from the baking will kill any residual bugs in the dirt, it's nicer not to eat it. Some will insist the skin be salted oiled or pricked or wrapped in foil – be grateful for my idleness – I insist you do nothing.

Turn the oven down to 180°C and bake the potatoes on the middle oven rack for 1 hour. Give the potatoes a little squeeze to check the skin is crunchy and the insides fluffy. If not return to the oven for a further 15 minutes. The stickiness, inherent in a microwaved potato, will instead have turned into sweet, warm, potato comfort.

Split the potatoes and fill with more butter, oil, non-dairy spread than you should; potatoes love it and so will you. Flavoured oils such as chilli, basil or nut oils can be used if you're feeling racy. I've never really understood why jacket potatoes feature so predominately in 'diets', if you're not topping your potato in luscious, rich fats and goodness, there really is no point.

Ideal for feeding a crowd, as the preparation is minimal. A good jacket potato can sop up the juices of stew, bolognaise sauce, chicken curry, chilli or a slow-cooked meat. Cheese begins to melt when it meets a hot potato's insides; I've yet to find a cheese that doesn't enjoy this contact.

If salty is your thing, mash in a heaped teaspoon of tapenade and chopped fresh tomatoes. The possibilities are endless - roasted vegetables and goats cheese, crisp bacon and tomatoes on a bed of crisp lettuce, tuna with crunchy radishes and cucumber, aubergine dip and wilted spinach, a mashed can of sardines in tomato sauce.

Making An Effort

Making an effort should not be confused with 'difficult', 'fiddly' or 'arduous'. Making an effort is when you either have a little more time to organise yourself or are feeding others. It may be an occasion where none of the meal has a 'leftover' constituent or when you don't need to be somewhere else within 15 minutes of laying the table. I have also included anything that takes over 30 minutes to cook, even if you are not physically required to be in the kitchen.

Food that requires deep-frying is terribly quick and easy to do, but I have it in the making an effort category, as it requires your undivided attention. Some food just needs a bit more time to have a think. Long-marinated or long-baked food spends most of its time just sitting having a think, before a very quick burst of activity. Again, not difficult but time can be a precious commodity during a disorganised period.

Lastly, I come to food that you may not normally use. For the most part my cooking generally revolves around the store-cupboard or freezer. The effort required for some of the following recipes, may simply be that you remember to buy the ingredients.

Slow Cooker

Slow Cookers are immensely useful. They will quietly turn a jumble of vegetables and meat into a meal that hugs you from the inside and you don't even have to be present! What a generous piece of equipment. I have a 6.5l slow cooker, the large size means you can cook a large batch and the oval shape takes longer cuts of meat. You will need to half the recipe for a smaller cooker.

If you are in the market for a slow cooker may I suggest you buy one with a metal dish? A lot of IBS patients have clumsy tendencies and it is a lot harder to smash a metal bowl - replacement ceramic bowls are surprisingly tricky to find. The metal dish may not be as attractive to bring to the table but you benefit from being able to sear the meat first in the same pan.

Making An Effort

The recipes that follow for pulled chicken, pulled pork and brisket all have the same serving suggestions – serve on tacos, rice noodles, mashed potatoes, in lettuce cups, boiled rice, jacket potatoes or on the side of a salad. Leftover meat can make for a satisfying packed lunch or mixed with leftover mash and fried in patties.

Each has its own sauce and while we would eat this with the meat, I put any leftover sauce to good use as a base for a soup.

A Word on Deep-frying Food

I use a pan of oil for deep-frying, as I haven't the space for a deep-fat fryer. When using the pan do not fill the oil more than one third of the way up the pan, ensuring there is at a very least, a 10cm gap at the top. I use either sunflower, vegetable, rapeseed or groundnut oil.

A heavy based pan is safest, but keep the handle turned away from you, so that it is not accidently knocked. Stability is key to safe deep-frying; do not move the pan once the oil is hot.

Deep-fried batter-clad food should be crisp not greasy with a tender, steaming centre. When frying in small batches keep a plate lined with plenty of paper kitchen towels warming in the oven, ready to transfer the fried food. Do not be tempted to pile the food too high without further paper towels - you want any excess oil to drain away from the food. It is also worth noting that I find it easiest to turn any food by using wooden tongs or a wooden spatula.

I use a thermometer to check the temperature; be careful not to overcrowd the pan as this will make the temperature drop.

If the oil starts smoking, it is too hot. Turn off the heat and leave it to cool – **do not try to move the pan.**

If you consider yourself a nervous deep-fryer, do take a minute to follow the advice on any fire service website and think about buying a fire blanket.

Fruity Ribs

Serves 4

Prep - 15 mins + Marinating time - 3-8 hours

Cooking - 40 mins

1.5kg baby-back pork ribs

750ml cranberry juice

Juice of 1 orange

Juice of 1 lime

Juice of 1 lemon

25g root ginger, peeled and thinly sliced

3 star anise

2 cinnamon sticks, broken in half

½ tbsp. Szechwan peppercorns

⅛ tsp. asafoetida

¼ tsp. chilli flakes

1 tsp. coriander seeds

Pinch of salt flakes

Unapologetic in my love for gnawing meat off bones, I give you the ultimate in gnawing fun – ribs. These are a fruity-flavoured, tender, baked rib, as opposed to a barbequed variety. Ideal for a British summer's day – one that is too rainy to fire up enthusiasm, let alone a barbeque. The overall effort involved in this dish is minimal.

Please don't be put off by the large amount of fruit juice needed for marinating – it's not all eaten. The marinating time is not prescriptive, it's as long as you have time for.

Place the ribs in a large pan and cover with boiling water. Boil for 10 minutes.

Mix all the remaining ingredients in a large bowl. Drain the ribs and place them in the marinade. Turn the ribs over until everything is covered in juice. Cover and refrigerate. If you get the opportunity to turn the ribs over during the marinating time then do so.

Remove the ribs from the fridge and preheat the oven to 190°C. Tip the ribs and marinade into a large roasting tin with the bones facing up. Allow the meat to come up to room temperature while the oven heats. Cover the tin with foil and bake for 30 minutes. Take the tin from the oven, remove the foil and turn the ribs over so that they are now bone side down. Turn the temperature up to 200°C and return to the oven uncovered, for 10 minutes.

Remove the ribs to a warm serving dish and strain all the residual marinade into a small pan. Reduce the sauce for 5 minutes, place in a jug to pour over the ribs as you serve. Serve with plenty of napkins.

Scallops with Fennel, Lemongrass and Bacon

Serves 4

Prep and cooking – 15-20 minutes

12 scallops cleaned and sliced in half horizontally, retain the roes.

6 slices thick cut back bacon cut into 1cm strips

200g coconut cream

Handful of fresh coriander roughly chopped

1 lime

1 stalk lemongrass, bashed, outside tough leaves removed and the inside finely shredded

150g (½ bulb) fennel, finely diced

2 tbsp. olive oil

Scallops would probably feature somewhere in my last meal. I like the roe and feel cheated when an over-officious chef has removed it – that was mine, give it back! Apart from the flavour, roes bring jolts of colour to an otherwise bland looking bit of seafood. If you like things a little livelier, finely chop half a small red chilli and add with the fennel. You can substitute the coriander for flat leaf parsley.

Fry the bacon in a wide shallow pan with 1 tbsp. of oil until lightly browned. Remove the bacon from the pan and set aside. In the same pan add another ½ tbsp. olive oil, turn the heat to medium high and add the fennel and lemongrass to soften.

When the fennel has softened, remove it from the pan and warm the last ½ tbsp. of oil. Turn up the heat cook the scallops and roes for 2 minutes on one side until they are starting to caramelise.

Gently turn the scallops, grate over the lime zest, add the bacon back to the pan and pour in the coconut cream. After 2 minutes, add the fennel and lemongrass, juice of half the lime and coriander, gently turning everything over to combine. Remove from the heat.

Serve with a pile of steaming rice and a green salad lightly dressed with olive oil and the juice from the other half of the lime.

Pizza

Makes 8 small pizzas.

Prep - depending on your chosen toppings, 15 minutes

Cooking - 30 minutes

180 ml coconut milk

1 tsp. lemon juice

550g self-raising gluten-free flour

¼ tsp. Xantham Gum

1 tsp. gluten free baking powder

¼ tsp. salt

1 tsp. caster sugar

180 ml fridge-cold soda water

1 tbsp. olive oil

Drizzle of olive oil

Extra gluten-free plain flour for dusting

You will need plenty of cling film or non-stick paper, rolling pin, 2 baking sheets lined with silicone or non-stick paper.

Toppings

Friday night is PIZZA NIGHT! At least it is in our house. I was never a fan of massive deep pan pizzas, which is lucky as these are definitely of the thin and crispy variety. In the interest of crispy bottoms and clean shirtfronts, I must insist you don't 'over-top' your pizzas.

For the base I use either the roasted veg sauce (see Roasted Vegetables and their uses) about 2-3 tbsp. per base, but you can simply blitz a can of chopped tomatoes with a handheld blender. If you would prefer not to use a sauce, cover the base with sliced tomatoes.

Toppings that we enjoy are chilli flakes, roasted vegetables, salami, pancetta, blanched spinach, feta, roasted aubergine, mozzarella, goat's cheese, ham, tuna, olives, capers, and anchovies... The world is divided between those who think pineapple on pizza is an abomination or the best thing ever – my mum and son are on opposite sides of this divide.

Preheat the oven to 240C, move both shelves near the top of the oven, leaving enough space to take the pizzas in and out without losing the topping.

Warm the coconut milk to body temperature either in a small pan or microwave. Stir in the lemon juice and set aside; it will look slightly curdled. Sift all the dry ingredients together in a large bowl and make a well in the centre.

Stir the milk then pour with the oil into the dry ingredients. Add the soda water; mix together using a wooden spoon and then a clean hand. It will turn into a sticky but smooth dough. Split the dough into 8 equal pieces, around 115g each.

Lay a sheet of cling film onto a work surface. Dust the cling film with flour and lightly knead a piece of dough between your palms. Shape into a ball and place in the centre of the sheet of dusted cling film. Lightly dust the top of the ball with flour and cover with a second sheet of cling film.

Pizza

Using a rolling pin, start rolling the ball, changing direction with each roll to keep an even shape. When the pizza is around 18 cm diameter, move it onto a baking sheet. The bases are very flimsy so my preferred way to move them is to remove the top sheet of cling film and slide my hand under the bottom sheet.

Flip this onto the lined baking sheet in one movement. You won't always get it right but you will get better with practice! Each sheet should take 2 bases. Repeat until you have 4 bases.

Top the pizzas and finish with a small drizzle of oil – chilli or flavoured oil is great. Bake the pizzas for up to 14 minutes, until the base is crisp and the top is bubbling. While the first pizzas are cooking, you can roll the rest of the bases, layering with cling film as you go.

Remove the cooked pizzas to a plate and drizzle the cooked pizzas with a little olive oil. Rocket, pine nuts, herbs or Parma ham are best added after cooking.

Polenta Chips

Prep - 20-25 minutes,

Chilling time - 2-8hrs

Baking - 20 minutes

Serves 4

5 tsp. olive oil

800ml boiling water

200g instant polenta

1 tsp. finely chopped rosemary

½ tsp. salt flakes

¼ tsp. ground black pepper

Optional 2 tbsp. finely grated pecorino or Parmesan cheese

Optional 50g grated firm cheddar-style cheese

It may seem strange to give you a recipe for a substitute when chips are one of the few things we can readily eat. However, it would be churlish to keep the recipe for these crunchy, oh-so-more-ish treats to myself.

"I have no time to make my own polenta!" I hear you cry. Fair enough, there is a second recipe, using a ready-made polenta block but the ready-made method will mean you miss out on the surprising delight that can be found in slapping hot polenta.

The recipes do contain suggestions for further variations but these are my initial thoughts - you can substitute the rosemary for fresh sage, thyme or a mixture of all three: I wouldn't use a more delicate leafy herb. Try using a flavoured, smoked or herbed salt, or change the black pepper for a long, pink or comet variety.

Polenta Chips from Scratch

I use instant, quick cook polenta and I can't say I would bother using the non-instant kind when I am going to bake it. I use the instructions on the side of the packet - if yours are wildly different to mine, I suggest you follow the manufacturers instructions. I heartily recommend adding the optional cheddar-style cheese; it adds richness to the chips. A pecorino or Parmesan coating will also add crunch.

Using a teaspoon of oil lightly grease a 28 x 18cm baking tray with 1 tsp. of oil.

In a large, high-sided pan, boil the water and slowly stir in the polenta with a wooden spoon. Keep stirring but please be aware it can splutter up and burn you.

Stir until the mixture is evenly thick and bubbling, around 5 minutes. Beat in the cheddar-style cheese, if using, until melted and then tip the polenta onto the baking tray. Spread out as much as possible with the back of a spoon. When the mixture is cool enough to touch lightly slap the top all over until it is all an even thickness and relatively smooth. Chill uncovered in the fridge for anywhere between 2-8 hours.

Polenta Chips

Ready Made Polenta Chips

Prep - 10 minutes

Cooking - 20 minutes

Serves 4

500g block of cooked polenta

3 tbsp. olive oil

Approx. 10 leaves of sage (if they look big use less)

Sea salt (Maldon flakes are ideal)

Black pepper

Optional 2 tbsp. finely grated pecorino or Parmesan cheese.

Pre-heat the oven to 200°C. Brush the top of the polenta with 2 teaspoons of olive oil before tipping the polenta onto a board, oiled side down. Brush the other side with 1 tsp. of oil, sprinkle with the rosemary, salt, pepper and pecorino if using. Cut into 'chips' or diamonds. This mixture will make around 33 depending on your accuracy when cutting.

Place the chips on a large baking sheet lined with a silicone sheet or parchment and greased with 1 tsp. of oil. Do not let the chips touch. Drizzle with the remaining teaspoon of oil. Bake for 20 minutes until golden and a little crunchy around the edges.

Bash the sage together with the oil in a mortar and pestle until the oil has taken on a green hue and the leaves are decimated.

Cut the block into thick chip sizes - cut the block in half horizontally, then each half into 1.5cm chips.

Pour the oil and sage onto a shallow baking tray, add the polenta chips, turn them over in the oil then space them evenly apart. Season well then bake for 10mins. Turn the chips over in the pan, sprinkle the Parmesan onto the top of the chips and return to the oven to cook for a further 10 minutes.

Serve in a bowl of if you're feeling fancy, stack in a Jenga style.

Slow-Roasted Belly Pork with Ras-el-Hanout

Prep - 5-10 minutes

Cooking - 4hours, 45 minutes + 15 minutes resting time.

Olive oil for greasing the pan

Juice of 2 limes

Juice of ½ lemon

Handful of thyme sprigs

2 kg piece of pork belly, boned, with well-scored skin

2 x heaped tbsps. ras-el-hanout

½ tsp. salt flakes

Pre-heat the oven to 110°C.

Universally loved by everyone who has tried it, this belly pork recipe is terrifically easy. It has a long cooking time when it is quite happy to quietly turn into a juicy meat-treat with very little attention. This is a good way to feed a hungry horde, when you are too busy attending to the hungry horde, to spend any length of time in the kitchen. If you are not feeding a horde do use a smaller piece of pork, although I prefer to have leftovers – cook once, feed twice.

This is not the only appearance of ras-el-hanout in this book - I really like it! There should be no garlic in the spice mix but do double check the ingredients.

Lightly grease a roasting pan large enough to take your piece of pork. Add the lemon, lime and thyme sprigs evenly to the pan.

Lay the pork skin side up on top of the thyme and dry the skin using kitchen towel. Using your fingers rub the ras-el-hanout into the skin, making sure it is also rubbed between the scores. Sprinkle salt flakes evenly over the skin. Place in the oven for 4 hours then turn the oven up to 140 for a further 45minutes.

Take the pork out of the oven, make a foil tent over the whole pan and allow the meat to rest for a further 15 minutes.

Remove from the tin onto a warmed plate, slice into juicy slices and drizzle with some of the pan juices. Cut into thick slices. If you wish to 'pull' the pork, remove the skin first. Simply run a sharp knife between the fat and skin, it is easiest to cut up the skin using sharp kitchen scissors. The meat will tease into juicy strands using two forks.

Kedgeree

Serves 4 (serves 6-8 if also making pakoras)

Prep and cooking - 45mins (although only 15 minutes are spent doing things).

450g smoked white fish (haddock, cod, coley etc.)

2 bay leaves

1 inch blade of mace

1 tsp. black peppercorns

700ml water

2 tbsp. sunflower oil

2 heaped tbsp. Low-FODMAP curry powder *(See Low-FODMAP Life Hacks)*

300g basmati rice

400ml canned coconut milk

Large handful of flat leaf parsley, roughly chopped

4 eggs at room temperature *(Optional, omit if you are unable to eat eggs.)*

Salt for seasoning.

If you were anything other than a man and part of the landed gentry, the Victorian era would have been fairly dreadful to live through but curried fish for breakfast, what treats! Knowing my luck, I probably would have been on the wrong side of the green baize door...

Kedgeree fills a good meal gap in the expanse between Christmas and New Year, some fish and spice when you simply can't face another platter of meat and cheese. The preparation time for this dish is fairly minimal – a couple of minutes activity then several bursts of inactivity. I usually make some pakora as an informal starter, not least because the kedgeree smells so divine whilst cooking that it is torturous not to have a little spicy something to nibble on.

Bring a pan of water to the boil, turn down the heat and lower in the eggs, ensuring they are covered by 1 inch of water. Simmer for 6 minutes. Remove from the heat immediately, and, using a slotted spoon, plunge the eggs into very cold water.

While eggs are simmering, place the fish in a wide lidded pan with the water, bay, mace and peppercorns. Cover, bring to a simmer and cook for 6-8 minutes until the fish is starting to flake. It will depend how thick your fish fillet is as to exactly how long this will take.

Using a slotted spoon, remove the fish from the water and set aside on a plate to cool. Strain the water into a jug removing the spices. Rinse out the pan and put on a medium high heat with the oil to warm. Add the spices to the oil and then the rice; stir until all the rice is well covered. Top up the reserved water to 700ml then pour into the rice with the coconut milk. Stir thoroughly, cover and bring to a simmer.

Simmer with the lid on for 10-12 minutes. Every few minutes stir the rice to ensure it doesn't stick. Lightly tap the eggs until the shells are all broken then peel away the shell under running cold water. Cut into halves or quarters and set aside. When the rice is tender remove from the heat. Break the fish into flakes by hand and add to the rice with the parsley, saving a little extra parsley to scatter over when serving. Season to taste – depending on how salty your fish was, you may not need any further salt. Serve from the dish onto warmed plates and top with the eggs.

Feta and Fennel Risotto

Serves 4

Cooking - 30 minutes

1 tbsp. garlic olive oil

1 tbsp. extra virgin olive oil

200g finely chopped fennel bulb

25g butter

300g Arborio rice

1 litre vegetable stock

Large pinch of sea salt flakes (preferably herbed)

For the baked feta cheese

1 tbsp. olive oil

200g block of feta

6-8 sprigs of oregano/ marjoram/ thyme

Freshly ground black pepper

Preheat the oven to 200°C.

Italians would rarely serve anything on the side of a white risotto but I think it can make a lovely background to seared fish or sitting upon piles of lovely wilted greens – the creamy white makes other colours pop. In this version, I used Baked Feta, omitting the tomatoes, stirred through at the end.

In a large heavy based pan warm the oil over a medium heat. Add the fennel, cover and soften for 5 minutes, stirring occasionally. Meanwhile, prepare the feta cheese, according to the **Baked Feta** recipe and start to bake for 15 minutes. Heat the stock.

Add the butter to the fennel; melt a little then stir in the rice. Stir for a minute, ensuring all the rice is glossy and covered in butter. Add a ladle of stock, stir until it has been absorbed and add another ladleful. Continue stirring and adding stock until the rice is creamy and cooked to 'al dente' but not chalky. It will take around 20 minutes.

Open the feta foil parcel, remove the herb stalks and break up the cheese with a fork. Tip into the risotto, and stir through plenty of black pepper. Serve with a sprinkle of finely grated pecorino or Parmesan.

Gnocchi

Serves 4

Prep and cooking 20-25 minutes

850g cold mashed potatoes made from jacket potatoes

150g gluten-free plain flour

Large pinch of salt

3 tbsp. extra plain flour for dusting and rolling

If there's a cooking shortcut to be found, I can usually find it. I love the cosy way a tummy full of gnocchi feels and I love that my family will cheerfully eat a trough-full when drowned in green cheese sauce but I loathe peeling potatoes. Using baked jacket potatoes cuts out the tedium of potato peeling and makes for a drier mashed potato - perfect for feather-light dumplings. The potatoes can be cooked way ahead of time; I would put them in the oven the night before with whatever else I'm cooking. As soon as they are cooked, cut in half horizontally, to let any extra steam escape.

1.5 kg of potatoes when baked will yield 850g of mashed potatoes. Refer to Baked Jacket Potatoes for cooking guidelines. Simply scrape the insides out into a bowl and mash. I use a handheld mouli to make the mash as smooth as possible but you can use a potato ricer or a lot of elbow grease. Lumps of any size are unwelcome in gnocchi.

Blend the potato, 150g plain flour and salt together in a large bowl using a wooden spoon. When the dough starts to come together, use your hands to ensure everything is fully blended and bring together into a tight dough. Split the dough into four.

Dust a work surface with a little flour. Take a quarter of the dough and shape into a fat sausage. Using both hands roll the dough from the middle out, keeping the width as even as possible. It will take quite a few rolls, be patient so that the dough doesn't fall apart. When the sausage is about 1.5cm in diameter cut into 3cm lengths.

Dust the dumplings with a little extra flour and set aside. Repeat with the rest of the dough. Warm a serving bowl for the cooked gnocchi. Bring a large pan of water to the boil then reduce to a high simmer. Drop a quarter of the dumplings into the water and cook for 1½ - 2 minutes, until the dumplings bob up to the surface. Remove and drain using a slotted spoon. Repeat with the rest of the dumplings.

Smother in butter, olive oil and black pepper. Alternatively use **pesto, green cheese sauce** or **tapenade**. I think a hefty serving of grated cheese is always welcome.

Stuffed Peppers

Serves 4

Prep - 15 minutes

Cooking - 40 minutes

200g basmati rice

4 large peppers

1tbsp olive oil plus a little extra for drizzling (or garlic oil)

1 small rib of celery finely chopped (max 48g)

A handful of chopped fresh herbs, I used oregano, marjoram and thyme (I wouldn't advise rosemary)

3 plump sundried tomatoes, finely chopped (max 32g)

20 small black olives, finely chopped

60g mixed seeds (eg. pumpkin, sunflower, chia, sesame, poppy)

100g fresh goat's cheese or a crumbly sheep's cheese

Salt and pepper to taste

Pre-heat the oven to 170°C.

Shirley Conran wrote in 'Superwoman' "Life's too short to stuff a mushroom". I agree, mainly because I really dislike mushrooms. However, I can only assume Shirley had never stuffed a mushroom; stuffing flat vegetables couldn't be easier, simply dollop stuff on top of other stuff.

A 'safe' Low-FODMAP serving of sundried tomatoes is 8g but if you are particularly sensitive to fructose, substitute with extra olives. The celery will come it at a low-FODMAP 'safe' 12g per portion but if you are particularly sensitive to polyols, it can either be omitted or substituted by a small courgette.

Boil the rice as per the instructions on the packet, drain and leave to cool a little. You may use two packets of the microwave basmati rice - cook according to the packet. You need 675g of cooked rice in total.

While the rice cooks cut the peppers in half lengthways. If you are clever enough to slice through the stem so each one has a pretty green bit still attached, then do so. De-seed the peppers and remove as much of the white pith as you can. Place cut side up on a roasting tin lined with foil. Drizzle a little oil (don't go overboard) over the top of the peppers and bake for 10 minutes. This will remove a little of the crispness before you stuff them.

Warm the oil in a large frying pan, add the celery to soften with the asafoetida. Add the tomatoes, herbs, olives and seeds to warm through before adding the cooked rice. Mix thoroughly, season to taste, then spoon the rice mixture into the pepper cavities. Crumble the goat's cheese on top, and then drizzle with a little oil. Bake for 30 minutes and serve with a green salad.

Feta Cheese variation

Bake a block of feta with tomatoes and a finely sliced red chilli (see **Baked Feta**) while the rice is cooking. Stir everything into the cooked rice with a handful of chopped herbs and black pepper. Do not add salt, the feta is salty enough. Stuff into the peppers and bake for 30 minutes at 170°C.

Celeriac and Walnut Gratin

Serves 8 as a side dish

Prep 10-15 minutes

Baking 1 hour

1.4kg celeriac (or thereabouts), peeled.

Juice of half a lemon

1 tbsp. garlic oil

40g butter

45g gluten-free plain flour

400ml canned coconut milk

190ml almond milk (unsweetened)

Freshly ground pepper

60g finely grated pecorino

60g broken walnut pieces

Large pinch of salt flakes

Small pinch of cayenne pepper

Small amount of butter for greasing foil

Set the oven to 220°C.

Although I always like the idea of celeriac, I hate peeling it. However, I have found slicing the peel off with a knife, as opposed to a peeler, makes the process bearable. For this reason the quantity is a little vague – 1.4kg makes around 1 kg of usable celeriac. This dish will come out looking quite brown - please don't be put off, it's delicious! One idea may be to put it in a jolly, bright oven dish and serve with lots of greenery. Another idea is to eat it blindfolded.

If you'd prefer a vegan dish leave out the pecorino and use a dairy-free spread instead of butter. This recipe deliberately makes a large dish as I always enjoy the leftovers for lunch the next day.

Fill a large pan with cold water and the lemon juice. Cut the celeriac into quarters and slice each thinly. Place the slices in the lemon-water to stop them browning.

Melt the butter in a pan over a medium heat. Add the flour and whisk together until it makes a smooth paste and has started to brown. Whisk in the almond milk until smooth before tipping in the coconut milk. Add the salt and cayenne pepper then continue to whisk together to remove any lumps until the sauce has thickened. Remove from the heat.

Grease the dish with the garlic oil; it is likely to stick around the edges. Drain the celeriac and place half in the dish in a roughly even layer. Spread half of the sauce and half of the nuts over the celeriac. Add the rest of the celeriac, then spread over the remaining sauce. Sprinkle the remaining nuts and pecorino evenly over the top. Grind over black pepper to taste. Grease a piece of foil and use it to securely cover the dish. Try not to let the foil touch the cheese or you will lose half of the crusty cheese when you remove the foil.

Bake for 50 minutes, remove the foil and grill under a medium heat for 5 minutes.

Brisket

Serves 8 as a meal or up to 16 as a taco filling.

Prep - 10 minutes

Cooking - 8 hours

1 whole dried ancho chilli

300ml boiling water

1 tbsp. coriander seeds

1 tsp. cumin seeds

½ tsp. fennel seeds

1 tbsp. sunflower oil or beef fat

2 kg. rolled beef brisket

1 tsp. dried oregano

1 tsp. dried thyme

½ tsp. freshly ground black pepper

400g tin of chopped tomatoes

¼ tsp. asafoetida

350g carrots, peeled and sliced

Very large bunch of fresh coriander

I seem to be giving you another brown recipe – sorry. Actually I'm not sorry. This is another taco filling triumph - you can jazz it up with some colourful vegetables as you fill the tortilla. Otherwise, a wintery day is made comforting when brisket is served with a pile of fluffy mashed potatoes and buttered spinach. It is not a Texan-style barbequed brisket but a more modest British-style rib-sticking meal.

There will plenty of leftover sauce that I freeze to eat as ready-made gravy with sausages. Any leftover brisket can be covered in sauce and frozen in portions. You can use a smaller piece of brisket but I wouldn't bother changing the proportions of the rest of the ingredients, as the sauce is useful in itself.

In a small bowl, cover the chilli with the boiling water and set aside. Later you will need to add the soaking water as well as the chilli.

Using either your metal slow cooker dish or a large frying pan, dry fry the seeds for a minute or two until they start to pop. Remove from the pan as soon as they are toasted. Heat the oil or fat in the slow-cooker dish or frying pan over a high heat and sear the brisket on all sides. Remove the pan from the heat and place the brisket on a plate.

Place all the ingredients, except the beef and fresh coriander into the slow cooker dish. Sit the beef on top and lay the fresh coriander over the top of the beef. Cook on a low setting for 8 hours.

Remove the beef from the dish and using a handheld wand blender, blend together everything left in the dish, including any leaf coriander still attached to the beef. Tip the sauce into a pan and warm through. Check for seasoning.

Serve the beef either in thick slices or chunks with the sauce poured over.

Pulled Pork with Chipotle

Prep - 5 -10 minutes + 15 minutes

Cooking - 8 hours

1.5kg - 2.5kg boneless pork shoulder, skin removed (*use the skin to make crackling*)

40g muscavado or dark brown soft sugar

½ tsp. ground cumin

1 tbsp. sweet smoked paprika

½ tsp. ground black pepper

⅛ tsp. ground white pepper

½ tsp. table salt

1 litre tomato juice

1 heaped tsp. diced dried chipotle flakes

30ml non-brewed condiment

Although pulled pork makes a delicious taco, it makes a divine bowl of noodles when stirred through freshly cooked rice noodles with coriander leaves. When buying the meat, ask the butcher to remove the skin from the pork and then re-string the meat. It's not essential but it makes life easier. Pork shoulder shrinks by around a third as it cooks; for a very large 200g serving you'll need 300g of raw meat. I have cooked both the smaller and larger amount pork using the same recipe. Please note a low-FODMAP portion of tomato juice is 200ml – share the sauce between at least 5 people!

Mix together the sugar, cumin, paprika, peppers and salt in a small bowl. Rub the mixture over the fat on the top of the pork. Place the pork into the slow cooker dish with the fat side up. Pour over the tomato juice and non-brewed condiment; add the chipotle flakes to the liquid and cook on a low setting for 8 hours.

Remove the meat to a large warm serving dish. Put the liquid into a pan and heat gently to reduce by a third. You will need to stir this often as it can splutter and redecorate your kitchen in burning-hot, red splashes. Remove the string from the meat and when the pork is cool enough to handle, pull apart with your hands. Stir half of the sauce over the meat and put the remainder in a jug to serve.

Pulled Chicken

Serves 6-8

Prep - 5 minutes + 15 minutes

Cooking - 6-8 hours

Spices

6 cm cinnamon stick, broken in 2

6 cm root ginger, sliced into discs

2 whole star anise

2 black cardamom pods, split and lightly crushed

1 tbsp. fennel seeds

1 tsp. szechwan peppercorns

2 bay leaves

1.25kg - 1.5kg whole chicken

450 ml chicken stock

60g carrot, sliced

1 heaped tsp. tomato puree

1 tbsp. maple syrup

Large pinch of salt flakes

Juice of 1 lime

The smell of warm spices and chicken cooking is scrumptious. Pulled chicken, much the same as the other slow cooked meats, makes a great taco or noodle topping but it also works really well on sandwiches. The prospect of getting that aromatic flavour and soft chicken texture between two slices of something gluten-free is too good an opportunity to miss.

I don't often get the opportunity to freeze any of this, as it all tends to get snaffled away. However, I do still benefit from leftovers by boiling the bones into a delicious Chinese-y flavoured stock for making noodle soup.

Place the spices in a dry pan (or metal slow cooker dish) over a high heat and toast for 30 seconds. Remove from the heat and add all the other ingredients. Cook over on the low setting for 6-8 hours. In honesty the chicken won't mind too much if you're an hour late back from work but you may need to add a little more stock to stop the chicken drying out.

Remove the chicken to a large warmed dish and cover with foil. Strain all the cooking liquid into a pan – there should be around 500ml. Reserve the spices if you would like to make a stock. Put the pan over a medium high heat to reduce by half. While it reduces, remove all the meat from the chicken. Pull the flesh into strips and stir in the reduced sauce to keep all the strands of chicken juicy.

For the stock, place all the bones and reserved spices into a pan and cover for 1.5 litres of water. Bring to the boil and simmer for 1.5 -2 hours. Strain and store.

Prawn Pakora

Makes approx. 20

Prep and cooking - 20 minutes

When you don't eat onions, it can be easy to dismiss Indian food altogether. I always have to remember Indian food is not just onions! Technically, these are not even remotely related to real pakora – there's no gram flour, onions, garlic or other pakora essentials, but when they are magma-hot from the oil and you need a spicy hit, I wouldn't worry.

1l sunflower oil for deep-frying (*see* Note on **Deep Frying** *in the chapter introduction*)

1 quantity Low-FODMAP **Mild Curry Powder** (approx. 50g)

175g gluten-free self-raising flour

75g rice flour

2 tsp. baking powder

2 heaped tsp. 'No-Egg' egg replacer

4 tbsp. water

250ml fridge cold soda water

Very large handful coriander leaves, chopped

225g cooked prawns, chopped into 1cm pieces

Sift the flour and baking powder into a bowl and mix in the curry powder. Start to heat the oil in a wide, deep pan to 180-185°C. Keep an eye on the oil while you make the batter.

Place the water into a separate smaller bowl, add the egg replacer and whisk until foamy. Make a well in the centre of the flour; pour in the egg replacer and soda water. Working quickly, whisk together until it is well blended. Fold in the coriander and prawns until thoroughly combined.

If you do not have a cooking thermometer, test the oil temperature by dropping in a cube of bread. When it bubbles and turns golden within 10 seconds, it is ready for frying.

Carefully drop a heaped teaspoon of batter into the oil, taking care not to splash yourself. Do not be tempted to fry more than 5 pakora at a time – the oil temperature will drop too much and the pakoras will have different cooking times. Fry for 1 minute on each side, turning with a slotted spoon. The pakora will turn a golden brown. Remove from the oil and put to drain on a warmed plate covered with kitchen towel in a low oven. Continue with the rest of the batter. Always put layers of kitchen paper between the pakora to drain the oil away.

Serve warm, if not hot, as they are, with lemon wedges and/or fresh chopped green chillies, and/or tomato chilli sauce.

Cockles and Spinach

100g spinach, wilted, water squeezed out and roughly chopped

180g cooked cockles.

Substitute the prawns and coriander with spinach and cockles. I have a fondness for cockles - a huge seaside flavour in a tiny package with a happy name. Do not use cockles in vinegar, it will be revolting.

Spicy Aubergine Fritters

Makes around 36 slices

Prep - 30 minutes
salting + 10 minutes

Cooking - 15-20
minutes

1l sunflower oil for
deep-frying (*see* Note
on **Deep Frying** *in the
chapter introduction*)

300g aubergines sliced
into 3-5mm discs
(around 36 slices)

30g table salt

170g gluten-free plain
flour

140ml fridge-cold soda
water

70ml coconut milk

2 tbsp. Low-FODMAP
Mild Curry Powder

For the Raita
120g of goat or sheep's
yogurt stirred to
loosen.
80g of coarsely grated
cucumber **or** 70g of
banana quartered
lengthways, then thinly
sliced.

An egg, gluten, cow's milk free, Low-FODMAP diet doesn't typically lend itself to battered food. Light tempura can be a pleasant change but sometimes you need a heftier, chip-shop style batter. These little fritters are delicious fresh out of the pan although you may have to beat off little pickers from eating them all before you have finished frying.

Salting the aubergine first will make the slices slightly floppier – no bad thing when you are trying to flip the slices about in batter. Do make sure you thoroughly rinse off all the salt and dry properly or it tastes like you are eating a salt lick. At the end is a recipe for simple raita dips.

Place the aubergine in a colander and toss with the salt. Leave to stand for 30 minutes.

Rinse the aubergine slices thoroughly under cold running water. Lay a clean tea towel on a work surface and cover one half with lots of paper kitchen towels. Lay the aubergine slices onto the kitchen towel and fold over the other half of the tea towel to dry the slices, pressing down lightly.

Start heating the oil. Sift the flour into a bowl and using a balloon whisk, stir in the curry powder. Make a well in the centre of the flour and pour in the soda water and milk. Using the balloon whisk bring everything together into a smooth batter. Check the temperature of the oil. When the oil reaches 180°C or a small piece of bread bubbles and turns golden within 10 seconds, it is ready for frying.

Dip the aubergine, one piece at a time, into the batter. Ensure it is all covered and wipe any excess batter off on the inside edge of the bowl. Gently slip, one slice at a time, into the hot oil. Do not cook more than 5 slices at a time: the slices should not be touching.

Fry for 1 minute on each side before removing with a slotted spoon. Place on a warm plate lined with plenty of kitchen paper. Check the temperature of the oil and repeat with the rest of the slices.

Raita

Mix the ingredients together, ready to dollop on the warm aubergine slices.

Hake Cakes

Serves 4 as light meal (makes 12 cakes)

Prep and cooking - 25 minutes

100g carrots, peeled and roughly chopped

1 small red chilli, deseeded and roughly chopped

450g hake or other firm fish

Very large handful of basil leaves

Pinch of sea salt flakes

2 tbsp. rice flour

1 tbsp. cornflour

Groundnut oil for frying

Hake cakes - rhyming food is fun. Well it is in my world. These little lightly-spiced fish cakes are easy to make, even easier if you get a spare pair of hands to help you shape the cakes. Eat dipped into Sweet and Sour Chilli Sauce.

You can use any firm fish, cod, salmon, haddock, pollock or even raw prawns etc. but it won't rhyme; the choice is yours.

Blitz the carrot, basil, salt and chilli in a food processor until tiny. Dab the fish dry with a kitchen towel then add to the processor and blitz until it forms a rough paste. Add the flours and give a final brief blitz until everything is combined. With your hands, make a walnut sized ball of paste and squash slightly to form a little patty.

In a large heavy-based frying pan, heat 3mm of oil over a medium-high heat. Carefully add the patties, taking care not to overcrowd the pan. Be careful, the oil can get terribly lively so turn it down if it is starting to burn the cakes. After 4 minutes gently turn the cakes and cook for 2 minutes on the other side. Do not attempt to move the fish cakes until a thick crust has formed on the bottom.

Remove onto a warmed plate lined with kitchen paper and leave in a warm place while you cook the next batch. A crisp side salad can act as a good foil to these rich little morsels.

Satay Skewers

Serves 4

Prep - 20 minutes

Marinating time 1-8hrs

Cooking - 10 minutes

20g peeled grated ginger

1 tbsp. garlic oil

3 tbsp. coconut aminos or light soy sauce

Grated zest of ½ lime

⅛ tsp. ground white pepper

500g beef skirt steak, trimmed of membranes

Sunflower or groundnut oil for basting

Optional ½ tsp. chilli flakes

Place 20 bamboo skewers in a baking tray of water.

Meat on a stick is surely one of the oldest and most obvious ways of cooking and eating meat – it keeps your hand out of a fire and small pieces cook quickly. These days we have the luxury of grills but I still like the basic nature of skewering food. Ideally, these would be made with goat meat but I know this can still be tricky to find; lamb shoulder would be a good substitute. Sadly, I can't tolerate it, so use beef instead. The meat needs to be slightly fatty to self-baste as it cooks. I use a skirt cut of beef and enjoy the endless amusement of asking the butcher for 'a nice bit of skirt'. You can use chicken thigh meat but it can be dry – add another tablespoon of oil to the marinade and baste often during grilling. If you can tolerate it, the coconut aminos can be substituted for Low-FODMAP light soy sauce.

If you prepare double the amount of meat, you can freeze half before leaving to marinade. Remove from the freezer to the fridge 8 hours before cooking and the meat will marinate as it defrosts. A side portion of boiled rice is a natural partner to these skewers as are grilled vegetable kebabs. I suggest using sturdy vegetables that can tolerate being skewered and dunked.

Using a sharp knife slice the beef into ribbons about 10cm long and 1cm wide; it is easier to do the 1cm cuts across the grain of the meat.

In a medium bowl whisk together the remaining ingredients, excluding the sunflower oil. Add the beef and turn it over in the marinade until it is fully covered. Leave to marinade in a cool place for an hour. If you are marinating for longer, cover the bowl and place in the fridge.

When the marinating time is up, remove the skewers from the water. Thread the meat onto the skewers. For even cooking the meat should be threaded evenly and not bunched up.

Grill the skewers either on a grill pan, barbeque or overhead grill. Brush the bars of the pan, rack or grill with oil first and then cook for 3-4 minutes on each side, basting with sunflower oil before turning.

Serve with satay sauce either poured over the top or in individual bowls.

Satay Sauce

Serves 4

Prep - 15-20 minutes

Cooking - 20-30 minutes

200g roasted peanuts (rinsed and drained if salted)

1 tsp. garlic oil

2 tsp. palm sugar

Juice of a lime

150g canned coconut milk

60ml coconut milk

1 ½ tbsp. coconut aminos

½ tsp. chilli flakes

50ml water

Satay skewers with thick peanut sauce are yet another taste of home – a meal for family celebrations and sharing with others. My mum's sauce was an authentic recipe picked up from her time in Borneo, rich with onions and garlic. Alas, since waving a fond farewell to onions and garlic, the authentic recipe is but a distant delicious, memory. Undeterred, I give you my authentic Low-FODMAP version of satay sauce. Dip skewers of grilled meat, fish or vegetables into your own personal pot – it is utterly addictive, I'm pretty sure you could shoehorn satay sauce into any meal. We once ate satay sauce poured over popcorn – I'm still not entirely sure how I feel about this serving suggestion.

Consider doubling or tripling the recipe to freeze some portions – heated sauce stirred into rice noodles with some quickly chopped crunchy vegetables, is a meal in moments. Add a splash of water when you are reheating the sauce. It is easier to source roasted salted peanuts than unsalted ones: I simply wash the salt off using a sieve and leave to drain. You can add extra or remove the chilli to taste. If you can tolerate soy sauce, substitute the coconut aminos with a Low-FODMAP soy sauce.

Blitz the peanuts in a food processor for 20 seconds, scrape down the sides using a spatula and blitz again until the peanuts resemble breadcrumbs.

Warm the garlic oil in a pan over a medium heat. Add the remaining ingredients except the water and stir until thoroughly mixed. Stir in the water and bring to the bubble. Stir again (taking care not to get splashed by the sauce!), cover and reduce to a **very** low simmer for 20-30 minutes, stirring occasionally to ensure it doesn't stick. The sauce will darken slightly - this is good. Serve warm.

Sweet Stuff and Nonsense

Do you have pudding or dessert in your house? On the rare occasions when I get around to doing a two-course meal for the family, it brings me a certain sense of wellbeing and satisfaction.

Puddings can be an opportunity to have your low-FODMAP recommended one portion of fruit - on lazier, less competent days, a piece of fruit **is** pudding. Cold days require something warm and carb-rich to fend off the chill, hot days require something altogether more refreshing.

Baking is often the first thing to fall by the wayside on a restricted diet – no gluten, no eggs, and no milk – that's most baking ingredients gone! I have missed seasonal baked treats far more than I expected – putting up the Christmas tree and not celebrating with a warm mince pie was hard. A birthday party without a chocolate crispy cake was soul-destroying and a rainy Sunday afternoon teatime without a crumble was miserable.

Not to fret dear readers, I've done the experiments and alchemy, turning out countless flat, hard, baked products so that you don't have to. You too can have your seasonal spirits lifted with an 'almost' or 'lookalike' recipe!

Although I am very sugar-aware for my family and limit the amount of sweet stuff we eat, the benefit of cooking everything from scratch is that we have no hidden sugars. I know how much sugar is being eaten everyday and I loathe the idea of sweeteners We eat sugar and enjoy sweet treats but not everyday and certainly not for every meal. Dare I say the 'M' word? There is no magic solution; it's all about Moderation.

Banana Pancakes

Serves 4

Prep - 10 minutes

Cooking - 10-15 minutes

200g peeled ripe banana (about 2 medium bananas)

250g gluten-free self-raising flour blend

1 x heaped teaspoon baking powder

4 tbsp. sunflower oil

1 tsp. vanilla extract

160 ml coconut milk

½ tsp. ground cinnamon *(optional)*

Dairy-free spread for frying - I have tried oils, butter, coconut oil but nothing works quite as well as vegan margarine. Start out with a teaspoon and add more with each batch.

Banana pancakes have become our Saturday morning staple. It is the one day of the week when we don't have to be anywhere and pyjamas can stay on for a little longer. There is no sugar in the batter; our sugar comes with the toppings! We've eaten them with jam, maple syrup, butter, bacon and fruit, sometimes all at the same time. I tried to eek out a little extra lie-in by making them the night before but they really weren't the same as fresh. Very over-ripe bananas don't agree with the Little Miss and I but if they agree with you and you have some you need to use up - go for your life! The recipe makes around 16, depending on your generosity with the tablespoon.

Using a handheld blender, whizz the bananas to a puree in a bowl. Beat in the oil, vanilla extract and milk until smooth. In a larger bowl, sift the flour, baking powder and cinnamon (if using) together.

Pour the wet ingredients into the dry and mix until thoroughly combined. If your bananas are not terribly ripe, you may need to add an extra splash of coconut milk. Heat a wide frying pan and melt the dairy-free spread over a medium heat. Dollop the mixture in tablespoon heaps, leaving space between each pancake. Flatten the pile with the back of the spoon.

Fry until the bottom is browned for 3-4 minutes before turning. Do not be tempted to turn up to a high heat, as the sugar in the bananas will cause them to burn easily. Remove to a warmed plate while you continue with the rest of the batter.

Chocolate Pots

Prep - 5-10 minutes

Chilling - 1 hour

40g of 74% cocoa dark chocolate

45g coconut cream

One of the following flavourings:

1 tsp. vanilla extract + 10 fresh blueberries for the bottom of the pot

1 tbsp. crème de framboise + 5 fresh raspberries for the bottom of the pot

1 tbsp. strong espresso with a chocolate coffee bean to decorate

½ tsp. smoked sea salt flakes (do not add until the chocolate has been whisked)

A little pot of dark, intense pleasure, these chocolate pots can make you blush in the way that only the richest chocolate can.

This is a terribly easy dessert to make for a lot of guests, as there's virtually no skill or last minute preparation involved. I've given you the recipe for one portion so you can multiply as necessary. You could miss out the whisking stage as it is not a mousse but the whisking cools the chocolate evenly and tends to make a smoother pot.

Blitz the chocolate to smithereens in a food processor. Place a bowl over a pan of boiling water so it sits clear from the water. Add the coconut cream and chocolate. As the cream warms and the chocolate melts, remove from the heat and stir in your flavouring of choice. Using an electric hand whisk, whisk for 3-5 minutes. Tip into your little pots of choice, cover and chill in the fridge for 1 hour. If you chill for over an hour you will need to remove from the fridge for ½ hour before serving.

Rhubarb and Pecan Crumble

Serves 8

Prep - 20 minutes

Baking - 35 minutes

1 kg washed and trimmed rhubarb, sliced into 1.5cm pieces

1 heaped tbsp. golden caster sugar

4 tbsp. water

250g gluten-free plain flour

125g cold butter, cut into small cubes

100g crushed pecan nuts

2 tbsp. light brown soft sugar

In the world of amateur dramatics I was told that in order to look convincing when you are part of a 'chattering' crowd scene you should be mutely mouthing 'rhubarb and custard'. Or so I was told. Sadly, my days treading the boards amounted to little more than part of a chorus or peasant-y crowd scene. Maybe I was just too good at mouthing rhubarb and custard – they needed my skills as part of the mumbling great unwashed.

I digress. Rhubarb crumble with a nudge of pecan nuts, eat with custard. This is a large crumble because frankly, there's no greater gift than leftover crumble.

Pre-heat the oven to 180°C and butter a deep baking dish. My dish is 18cm x 28cm. Tip the rhubarb, caster sugar and water into the dish and bake for 15 minutes, stirring halfway through and topping up with another tablespoon of water if it is beginning to stick.

While the rhubarb bakes, sift the flour into a large mixing bowl. Using your fingertips, rub the butter into the flour until it resembles breadcrumbs. Stir in the sugar and pecan nuts.

When the rhubarb is baked, remove from the oven, tip the crumble topping evenly over the top of the rhubarb and return to the oven for 35 minutes, until the top is golden and a tiny bit crusty.

Custard

Serves 4

Prep - 10 minutes

3 tbsp. custard powder

350 ml almond milk

150 ml coconut milk

2.5 tbsp. caster sugar

I think I'd agree to eat anything if you promised to serve it with lashings of custard. Such a strange turn of phrase, 'lashings of custard' – lashings should be a negative thing! Custard and ginger beer are the exception to the lashing rule; the pleasure derived from these two only increases with the volume available.

Bird's custard powder does not currently contain egg, dairy or gluten but do check the ingredients. You can substitute the sugar for brown sugar if you fancy a caramel edge to your custard.

In a basin large enough to hold the milk, mix the powder and sugar to a smooth paste with a little of the almond milk. Warm the remainder of milks together in a pan.

When the milk is almost boiling pour it over the custard paste and whisk together. Return everything to the pan and heat over a medium-high heat, stirring continually, for up to five minutes until the custard has thickened. Pour into a jug and lash away.

Fairy Cakes

Prep - 15 minutes

Baking - 25-30 minutes

Makes 12

120g dairy-free sunflower margarine

120g caster sugar

120g gluten-free self-raising flour, sifted

2 heaped tsp. 'No-egg' egg substitute

4 tbsp. water

1 ½ tbsp. coconut milk

1 tsp. vanilla extract

Pre-heat the oven to 175°C. Line a 12-hole muffin tin with paper cases.

The ultimate in birthday party catering - Low-FODMAP, vegan and even better, they look and taste like birthday cakes! Fortunately, they can be made very quickly for cake emergencies. Unfortunately, they can be made far too quickly for what turns out was only a perceived cake emergency. In these situations I find it best to eat the evidence of your mistake as quickly as possible.

If you are an egg-eater by all means use two large eggs instead of the egg-substitute. The 'No-egg' will give a slightly chewy top that is actually very pleasant.

I have given you the basic recipe for the vanilla cakes and you can choose your favourite Butter Icing for the tops. I bake these in fairy-cake sized paper cases in muffin-sized tins – the sides of the tin support the cake shape better than a standard bun tin. I like the glitz of a shiny gold or silver case for birthday party food.

I am careful not to overfill the cases; there should be enough room for the icing. I do not pipe the buttercream on in a mountainous cupcake-swirl as I find the cake/icing ratio goes all out of whack and it is too sickly. A rough application with a palette knife is enough and far easier to disguise any damage that is created when transporting the cakes. At the end I have also given you our favourite raspberry and chocolate version.

In a mixing bowl using electric handheld beaters, whisk together the margarine and sugar. In a separate bowl, whisk together the 'No-egg' and water until thick and foamy. If you are using eggs instead, beat them together.

Add the 'No-egg' (or egg) to the margarine and sugar with 1 tbsp. of flour. Whisk together. Add the rest of the flour and whisk again. Finally whisk in the coconut milk and vanilla extract until it is a smooth dropping consistency. Split the mixture evenly between the paper cases. Bake for 25 minutes, check to see if the tops are springy you may need 5 minutes more. Remove from the tin to cool on wire rack.

Fairy Cakes

Our birthday version of these are the **raspberry and chocolate** cakes pictured.

Melt 30g of dark chocolate and pipe into shapes on a piece of greaseproof paper. Cover and put somewhere cool to set.

Add ⅛ tsp. natural raspberry extract to the cake batter with the vanilla extract.

Make raspberry **butter icing**, following the vanilla butter icing recipe but substituting the vanilla extract for ⅛ tsp. of raspberry extract. Whisk in 30g of mini chocolate chips at the end.

Ice the cooled cakes with the butter icing, place a fresh raspberry and some chocolate shapes on top and finally scatter over some freeze dried raspberry pieces with a flourish.

Also pictured is a **strawberry and chocolate** version – nothing more complicated than the standard fairy cake with **cocoa butter icing** and half a strawberry on top.

Butter Icing (4 Variations)

Coats a 20cm x 20cm cake or 12 generously coated buns.

Prep - 15 minutes

Vanilla Butter Icing

250g icing sugar, sifted

70g soft butter

1 tbsp. coconut milk

1 tsp. vanilla extract

During my first forays into baking, my cakes would be decidedly lacking in butter icing - not because I couldn't make it but because I had had 'a little taste'. Then another little taste, then another until there was only a thin smear left to sandwich a cake together. Happy days. Although I love my butter icing whipped to almost truffle-like airiness, I have very little patience for piped butter icing. I would rather spread thickly with a palette knife and get on with the more serious business of eating the butter icing.

I have given you the basic recipe for a basic vanilla butter icing with a few variations at the end. I can't say anyone has noticed my butter icing is made with goat's butter. You can freeze any leftover butter icing but you will need to re-whisk it once it is fully defrosted. Don't try to melt in a microwave, that's silly.

Butter Icing (4 Variations - Vanilla, Cocoa, Vegan Chocolate Peanut Butter, Blueberry)

Cocoa Butter Icing

Substitute the vanilla and coconut milk for 1 heaped tbsp. of cocoa blended with 2 tbsp. of coconut milk.

If you have a stand mixer, use that with the whisk attachment; otherwise use a handheld electric whisk and a large bowl.

Place the icing sugar and butter in the bowl that you will be whisking in. To limit the amount of flying sugar, use a wooden spoon to start blending the two together. When it starts to resemble a lumpy paste, you can start whisking on a low speed. Once everything is fully combined, mix in the vanilla extract and milk. Again on a low speed, continue whisking until everything is thoroughly combined.

Turn the speed up to high and whisk for 5 minutes until the butter icing is a barely-there pale yellow and a lighter-than-air-texture. Slather over your cakes and afterwards, do remember to lick the beaters.

Vegan Chocolate Peanut Butter Butter Icing

2 tbsp. peanut butter

60g dairy-free sunflower margarine

250g icing sugar

1 tbsp. coconut milk

30g dairy-free mini chocolate chips

Using a spoon, blend the icing sugar with the margarine. When it is mixed enough not to fly out of the bowl, add the peanut butter. Whisk on a low speed using electric beaters before adding the coconut milk and whisking until the icing is really light and fluffy. This will happen more quickly than it does using butter. Briefly whisk in the chocolate chips, cover the bowl and chill in the fridge for an hour before decorating cold cakes. The cakes will need to be kept cool to save the icing from melting.

Blueberry Butter Icing

Make as the vanilla icing but only add 1tsp. of coconut milk and do not add the vanilla. Toss in 50g of fresh blueberries and gently stir through. A few blueberries will burst but try not to over mix – too many burst blueberries will make the mixture too wet and it will split.

There are some excellent **natural extracts** available which can add a myriad of flavours to best complement your baking. Check the side of the bottle for quantities but you should only need a few drops.

Dairy-Free Sweet Orange Pastry

Makes 1 x 23cm tart tin or a 12-hole tart tin

Prep - 10 minutes

Chilling - 25 minutes

150g gluten free plain flour (plus extra for dusting)

35g vegetable shortening, broken into small lumps and chilled

40g coconut oil, broken into small lumps and chilled

Pinch of salt

1 orange, zest finely grated and juiced

1 tbsp. icing sugar

After my first few gluten-free pastry attempts I gave up. My longing for all things pie and tart related led me back to try again. Gluten-free pastry is fairly fragile but I recommend that you roll it between two sheets of cling film. This is a very useful and easy sweet pastry to have in your recipe and hosting checklist. A recipe that benefits from not only being free from most things but also vegan. That's another diet catered for!

Stir the little lumps of vegetable shortening and coconut oil through the flour until they are evenly coated. Cover the bowl and leave in the fridge for 10 minutes. Stir the salt into the orange juice and also leave that in the fridge for 10 minutes.

Tip the flour and fat into a food processor with the icing sugar and pulse in 5 second bursts until the pastry starts to form crumbs.

Add 1 teaspoon of orange juice, pulse again before adding another ½ teaspoon. The pastry may have come together in lumps. If it hasn't, add another scant ½ teaspoon of orange juice. Depending on your flour blend, it can take up to 3 teaspoons but only add ½ teaspoon at a time.

Turn out the pastry onto a very lightly floured piece of cling film and form into a fat disc. Wrap in cling film and chill in the fridge for 15 minutes. Do not over-chill your pastry as it will crack as it rolls.

Roll between floured sheets of cling film as your recipe dictates.

If you are making the **Mince Pie Lookalikes** you can use the remainder of the orange in the recipe.

Roasted Grape and Goats Cheese Tartlets

Serves 4

Prep - 15-20 minutes

Chilling - 15 minutes

Baking - 10 minutes

I invented ('invented' doesn't that sound grand?) this recipe for a French Night a friend was holding. This was to replace a fruit tart with cream but it goes further than that – it is both a cheese course and a dessert. This could equally be served as a light lunch or starter. Don't be put off by the savoury/ sweet juxtaposition, please try it, it's very lovely.

You will need 4 x individual loose-bottomed tart tins, lightly greased.

Pastry

150g gluten-free plain flour blend

75g very cold butter (goat for preference) cut into small cubes

2 tbsp. icing sugar

Roasted grapes

36 x large red seedless grapes

1 tbsp. olive oil

Small handful thyme, pref lemon thyme

Small pinch of salt flakes

Small pinch of freshly ground black pepper

Filling

200g mild soft goat's cheese

Finely grated zest of 1 lemon

1 ½ tbsp. icing sugar

Pre-heat the oven to 220°C. Place the all the roasted grape ingredients in a tin in a single layer and bake 10 minutes. Shake the tin halfway through to turn the grapes. Gently tip the grapes and juices into a bowl to cool.

Place the flour, icing sugar and butter into the bowl of a food processor and using the cutting blade, process in 10-second bursts until it resembles breadcrumbs. Add ice-cold water to the mixture a teaspoon at a time, pulsing for 10 seconds in between until the dough starts to come together as a ball. Depending on your flour blend, this can take up to 4 teaspoons.

Lay a sheet of cling film on a work-surface and tip the pastry onto it. Lightly knead the pastry together into a ball. Split into 4 and form each piece into a fat disc. Wrap each disc in cling film and place in the fridge for 15 minutes. Preheat the oven to 170°C.

Remove the pastry from the fridge. Place a sheet of cling film on the work-surface, put a pastry disc in the middle and cover with cling film. Roll out, turning the pastry a quarter-turn with each roll, to 3mm thick.

Carefully (the pastry is fragile) lay the pastry into a tin, lightly pressing up the sides until the tin is evenly lined. Use a knife to trim any excess pastry and with a fork, lightly prick the base and sides of the pastry. Repeat with the rest of the tins. Bake on a baking sheet in the oven for 15 minutes and then leave in the tins to cool.

Place the filling ingredients in a large bowl and using an electric whisk (or a stand mixer) beat until the cheese is whipped. Spoon the cheese mixture into the pastry cases and arrange 15 grapes on top of each tart. Drizzle over the grape juices and a few small thyme pieces. The tarts should be served marginally warm but not hot.

Mince Pie Lookalikes

Makes 12

On top of the pastry prep - Prep - 10 minutes

Baking - 15-18 minutes

1 orange

100g pecan nuts

35g dairy free margarine

65g maple syrup

50g candied orange peel, finely chopped

½ tsp. mixed spice

10g rice flour

1 quantity **Orange Pastry** (*see Low-FODMAP Life Hacks*)

A little coconut milk for glazing. Use 1 beaten egg if your diet allows.

Preheat the oven to 170°C. Grease a 12 hole tart tin. You can make this as one large tart in a 23cm loose-bottomed tart tin*.

Christmas can be a low-FODMAP minefield – a festival of dried fruit, almonds, gluten and everything drowned in either custard or rum. I used to make some amazing mince pies: making the mincemeat using homegrown apples, steeping it in 'I don't think I should drive' amounts of booze and maturing for a year. Sadly those days have gone but happily, I no longer spend Christmas as a bloated, pained wretch. I still make 'normal' mince pies for the rest of the family and visitors but I also came up with this lookalike. Frustratingly, this vegan alternative has really taken off, leaving me with a freezer full of 'normal' mince pies come January.

Grate the zest from the orange and squeeze the juice. Place the pecans into a large freezer bag and using a rolling pin, crush the nuts. Put the nuts in a bowl with the candied orange peel, rice flour, mixed spice and half the orange zest.

In a small pan, warm together the margarine, maple syrup and 2 tbsp. of orange juice then add to the nut mix. Stir the nut mix together until everything has combined and is starting to look like mincemeat. Cover the bowl and chill in the fridge. Make the pastry using the remaining orange juice and zest.

Lay a piece of cling film over your work surface and dust with flour. Place the pastry in the centre and sprinkle flour over. Be aware, if your pastry is too chilled or you hurry the rolling, it will crack. Cover the top with another sheet of cling film. Roll out the pastry gently between the films, turning the pastry a quarter turn with each roll.

When the pastry is an even 4 mm thick, remove the top layer of cling film and cut 12 bases: my tin takes a 7cm round. From the pastry scraps, cut 12 stars, kneading and re-rolling as necessary. Fill the cases evenly with the nut mixture.

Top the tarts with the stars and lightly wipe a little coconut milk or egg over each star. Bake for 15-18 minutes until the tops and edges are slightly browned. Leave to cool in the tray for 5 minutes before **very** gently removing to a wire rack. The pastry will be very fragile; you may find a small palette knife helps to lift them out.

*I will NEVER stop finding the phrase 'loose-bottomed tart tin' amusing.

Jam Tarts

Makes 12 tarts

Prep - 10 minutes

Chilling - 15 minutes

Baking - 16 minutes

1 quantity **Orange Pastry** (*see Low-FODMAP Life Hacks*)

150ml strawberry or raspberry jam

1 tbsp. coconut cream

Preheat the oven to 170°C. Grease a 12-hole tart tin.

You probably don't need me to give you a recipe for jam tarts but this is mainly here to remind you jam tarts exist. They are really quick and easy to make – a fresh homemade jam tart will knock spots off any of the dreadful commercially available ready-made jam tarts that abound. Although I find the mouthwateringly tangy version using marmalade delicious, on this occasion, I felt a traditional strawberry or raspberry tart was called for

Do be careful not to over-fill the tarts – if the jam bubbles over and sticks to the tin, you will be unable to remove the tart in one piece. I like to mix it up a bit and have some with, some without the star tops.

Roll out the pastry to a 3-4mm depth and using a 6.5cm cutter, cut out 12 tart bases. You can do this either rolling between two sheets of lightly floured cling film or a lightly floured work surface and rolling pin. Bring any scraps together and re-roll as needed. Cut out 12 2.5cm stars for the tops. Put the bases into the tin.

Beat the jam to loosen then put a scant teaspoonful in each tart. Top with a pastry star and wipe each star with a little coconut cream. Bake for 16 minutes, remove the tray from the oven and allow the tarts to cool in the tin for 5 minutes.

Very carefully, remove the tarts from the tin using a small flexible palette knife and place on a wire rack to finish cooling. Allow to cool completely before eating or the hot jam will take the skin from the roof of your mouth.

Chocolate Cornflake Cakes

Prep - 15-20 minutes

100g free from 'milk' chocolate

100g plain chocolate

30g butter (can substitute with coconut oil or non-dairy margarine)

1 tbsp. golden syrup

175g gluten-free cornflakes

Another recipe that saves the day when a birthday party comes calling, chocolate cornflake cakes are terrifically easy to make. You can either make them in 24 fairy cake cases, smaller mini cases or a mixture of both. Children love making them but be warned you may not have as many as you expected and your children will have very chocolatey mouths. The free-from 'milk' chocolate can be substituted for all plain chocolate or normal milk chocolate, if you can tolerate it. I often add a few drops of orange oil to the chocolate mix.

The cakes will keep in a cool place, in an airtight tin for a week. Try not to store them anywhere too accessible, it's far too easy to snaffle a mini-one as you walk past. We also have a frozen supply for emergency birthday party rations - they defrost in minutes.

Place the cornflakes in a large mixing bowl and line your bun trays or muffin tins with paper cake cases.

Break the chocolate into small pieces. Place a heatproof bowl over a pan of water that is on a very low simmer, making sure the water does not touch the bottom of the bowl.

Place the dark chocolate in the bowl first then add the butter, syrup and 'milk' chocolate. Avoid the temptation to stir the mix. When the chocolate is three-quarters melted, remove the bowl from the pan. Give it a gentle stir before allowing it to stand for a couple of minutes to allow the last of the chocolate to melt in the residual heat.

Stir until it is combined then pour over the cornflakes – I find a silicone spatula is the most effective tool. Stir until all the cornflakes are coated – it will look as though there isn't enough chocolate but be patient and keep mixing.

Spoon the mix into the paper cases and leave to set somewhere cool for an hour. Lick the spoon and bowl.

The Versatile Cake

Makes 16x 5cm x 5cm servings

Prep - 15-20 minutes

Baking - 30 minutes

6 tbsp. ground linseeds

9 tbsp. water

165g dairy-free sunflower margarine

165g caster sugar

165g gluten-free self-raising flour

½ tsp. baking powder

1 tbsp. coconut milk

Flavouring options

Vanilla - 2 tsp. vanilla extract

Chocolate - 2 tbsp. cocoa blended with 3 tbsp. coconut milk

Marble - 1 tsp. vanilla extract plus 1 tbsp. cocoa blended with 1.5 tbsp. coconut milk

Pre-heat the oven to 175°C. Grease and line a 20cm x 20cm baking tin.

The most versatile of cakes, this has one basic recipe that can either be flavoured with cocoa or vanilla. Our favourite is to make a marble cake, flavouring one half with vanilla and the other with cocoa. It is a really useful cake to bake when you are catering for lots of people or going somewhere and have been asked to bring something to add to the table. You can freeze pieces of the un-topped cake in an airtight container interleaved with greaseproof paper.

Flaxseeds are also known as golden linseeds and you can buy them ready ground or milled. If you are sensitive to high-fibre, don't get greedy and eat more than the recommended serving.

Stir the water and linseeds together in a small bowl, set aside to soak until gloopy. Using a handheld electric whisk, cream together the sugar and margarine until light and fluffy. In a separate bowl, sift the flour and baking powder together. Whisk a third of the linseeds into the creamed margarine and sugar. Whisk in a third of the flour, then repeat, alternating between linseeds and flour until all the mixture is combined.

If you are only making **vanilla cake**, whisk in the vanilla extract with the coconut milk, before pouring the batter into the tin and baking for 30 minutes.

If you are only making **chocolate cake**, whisk in the blended cocoa with the coconut milk, before pouring the batter into the tin and baking for 30 minutes.

If you are making **marble cake**, add the coconut milk and whisk again. Put half of the batter mix into another bowl. Flavour one half by whisking in the vanilla and whisk the cocoa blend into the other half. Simply put dessertspoon-sized splodges of the two batters into the baking tin, both on top and on the sides of each other. As it bakes it will even out.

Allow the cake to cool in the tin for 5 minutes before turning out onto a wire rack and removing the paper.

You can top the cake with **butter icing, chocolate** or **blueberry topping**. Blueberries work well with the slightly nutty flavour of the cake. With a myriad of butter icing flavours to choose from you need never produce the same cake twice!

Raspberry Cheesecake (+ Variations)

Serves 8

Prep - 20 minutes

Chilling - 1 hour then 2 hours

70g butter melted

225g low-FODMAP plain biscuits, crushed into crumbs

40g dark chocolate

2 sheets of leaf gelatine

150g soft goat's cheese

70g coconut cream

60g caster sugar

75g raspberries + 100g to decorate

A delightful addition to any tea table or party spread, a cheesecake says 'I've made an effort, I can do pretty cooking!' Cream cheese is a no-go on the Low-FODMAP diet because of all that pesky lactose: I've made my cheesecake using a soft goat's cheese. The amount of sugar and raspberries will eliminate any concerns you may have about a residual goat-y flavour but do use a firm cow's milk soft cheese if you'd prefer. There are many variations following the recipe but I do love the brown and pink colourway of this version, I make no apology for liking my biscuit base thick.

To keep the filling firm, this cheesecake needs to be kept refrigerated until serving.

You will need a 16cm loose bottomed cake tin (not a flan tin) I find a springform tin is the easiest get your baked goods out in one piece. Line the base and sides of your tin with non-stick baking paper so there are no gaps.

Melt the dark chocolate and butter in a bowl over a pan of simmering water. Place the biscuit crumbs in a bowl and stir in the chocolate and butter. Mix thoroughly then press into the tin in a tight and even layer. Cover with cling film and chill in the fridge for 1 hour until it is firm.

Break up each gelatine sheet into four, place in a small bowl and cover in cold water to soak for 10 minutes. Using an electric handheld mixer, whisk the goat's cheese to loosen. Warm the coconut cream in a bowl over a pan of simmering water. Squeeze the water from the gelatine sheets and drop into the coconut cream. Whisk immediately with the electric whisk until the gelatine has dissolved. Whisk in the sugar and tip the coconut cream mix into the goat cheese. Whisk again for 4 minutes until light and thoroughly combined.

Lightly squash the raspberries with the back of a spoon then stir into the goat cheese mixture. Pour onto the chilled base and even out the top with the back of a spoon. Cover with cling film and place in the fridge to chill for 2 hours to set. It is important you make sure your fridge shelf is level or your pink layer will look decidedly wonky, even wonkier than mine.

Raspberry Cheesecake (+ Variations)

Remove from the tin carefully and very gingerly unwrap the sides. Decorate with the raspberries either in precise concentric circles or randomly strewn across the top.

Cheesecake Variations

For a **blueberry cheesecake**, substitute the 75g of raspberries for blueberries and use cooled *Blueberry Topping* on the top. It is easier to put the topping on when the cheesecake is still wrapped in its baking paper and tin. Chill for another 30 minutes before removing.

For my ginger loving family I find using ginger biscuits for the base and 40g of finely chopped preserved ginger, drained of syrup, in the place of raspberries. Let everyone know it's a **ginger cheesecake** by decorating with small pieces of crystalised ginger.

Substitute the raspberries with strawberries to make a **strawberry and vanilla cheesecake**, adding a tsp. of vanilla extract into the coconut cream. Decorate with a high pile of sliced strawberries.

Blueberry Topping for Cakes, Cheesecakes and Desserts

350g fresh blueberries, washed but not dried

90g caster sugar

25g butter

2 tsp. lemon juice

1 tbsp. cornflour

You will be amazed at just how many kitchen disasters you can disguise with a good smothering of blueberry topping.

Place all the ingredients in a small, lidded pan and warm over a low to medium heat. Allow to cook through for 15 minutes, covered and stirring occasionally to stop the cornflour 'lumping'. As it heats the blueberries will start to burst. Uncover turn the heat up slightly and cook for a further 5 minutes stirring continuously. Allow to cool before using.

Welsh Cakes

Makes 20

Prep and cooking - 20 minutes

230g gluten-free self-raising flour + extra for rolling

1 tsp. mixed spice

15g dried cranberries, finely chopped

110g butter, very cold and cut into small cubes + extra for greasing

1 heaped tsp. 'no-egg' egg substitute

2 tbsp. water

80g caster sugar + 2 tbsp. for decorating

2.5 tbsp. coconut milk

Every St. David's Day when I make Welsh cakes I'm surprised just how quick and easy they are to make, they're also something the children can take the lead in preparing. A fresh, hot Welsh cake, will taste buttery, sweet, delicate and light; in my mind, any Welsh cake that is over an hour old is plain wrong. I don't have a traditional bakestone on which to cook my Welsh cakes but if you have a griddle, for authenticity's sake, please use it. Otherwise use a heavy based frying pan.

I have used a small amount of dried cranberries as I find them more tolerable than dried currants. We use goat butter, which seems apt for a Welsh cake. Who knows, now I've this version that is free-from our foibles, we could eat them all year round and not just March 1st.

Sift the flour and mixed spice into a mixing bowl. Rub the butter into the flour using your fingertips. When it has reached the texture of breadcrumbs, stir in the sugar and cranberries.

In a separate bowl, whisk the water and egg substitute together until foamy then stir the into the flour mixture with the coconut milk. Using a wooden spoon and then your hands, work the mixture into a smooth, soft ball of dough.

Lightly dust a work surface and rolling pin with flour. Roll out the dough to a ½ cm thickness. Cut out cakes using a 6cm cutter, drawing together and rerolling any scraps.

Heat your griddle or pan a high heat and wipe with butter. Cook the Welsh cakes for 2-3 minutes each side. The cakes will be quite delicate when cooking – try not to cook more than six at once so you have enough space to turn them without breaking.

The cakes will be brown but turn the heat if down they look like they are blackening. Once cooked, remove to a warm plate and dredge with the extra caster sugar – eat them while they're still warm. Dydd Gŵyl Dewi Hapus!

Gingerbread Muffin Cakes

Makes 12

185g peeled ripe banana

75g light muscovado or soft brown sugar

35g coconut oil (warmed to a liquid state)

40g sunflower oil

75g almond milk

1 heaped tsp. peanut butter

225g gluten-free plain flour

1.5 tbsp. baking powder

1 tsp. mixed spice

1 tsp. ground ginger

195g icing sugar

2 tbsp. lemon juice

Approximately 40g crystallised ginger to decorate

This recipe didn't start life as a gingerbread-muffin-cake; it was going to be something quite different that didn't go entirely to plan, so I covered my mistake in my favourite icing. The name came about later. I wasn't there when the cakes were happened upon and eaten but was greeted on my return by exclamations of how much they'd loved the gingerbread-muffin-cakes. So I stopped treating them as a mistake and embraced their squidgy loveliness.

I've given the measurements for the oils and milk in grams as it is easier to just weigh them straight into the banana, rather than fiddling about with measuring jugs and creating more washing up.

Preheat the oven to 180°C. Make sure you have a rack in the middle of the oven. Line a muffin tin with cupcake-sized paper cases.

Using a handheld blender purée the banana until smooth. Weigh in the sugar, coconut oil, sunflower oil, almond milk and peanut butter. Blend again until thoroughly combined.

Sift the flour, baking powder and spices together into a large mixing bowl. Make a well in the centre of the flour and pour the wet mixture into the dry, using a spatula to scrape out any last bits. Gently fold the mixture together with the same spatula until there are no floury bits left.

Spoon the mixture equally into the paper cases and bake in the middle of the oven for 20 minutes. Leave to cool in the tin for 5 minutes then transfer to a wire cooling rack.

When the cakes are completely cool, make the icing by blending together the icing sugar and lemon juice. Be patient when blending, it will come together but if you prematurely add more liquid, it will be come a dribbly mess. Ice the tops of the muffins using a teaspoon then decorate with the crystallised ginger, either in big pieces or small.

THE BEST Chocolate Chip Cookies (+ Ginger and Chocolate Chip Variation)

Makes 16

Prep - 10 minutes

Baking - 14 minutes

125g free-from sunflower margarine

75g caster sugar

50g soft light brown sugar

2 tsps. vanilla extract

200g self-raising gluten free flour blend

Pinch of salt

1 tsp. baking powder

2 tsps. almond milk

150g dark (semi-sweet) chocolate chips

Pre-heat the oven to 170°C. Line two baking sheets with greaseproof baking paper.

Do check your chocolate chips for any rogue high-FODMAP ingredients.

The best? Well yes, dear Fodmappers, I think so. As do all those who have eaten one and texted me a week later to say they're still thinking of its crisp yet squishy texture, soothing vanilla aroma and still-warm chocolate chip pleasures. It is rare to make such an all-encompassing free-from recipe that is so quick to whip up with relatively few specialist ingredients. As soon as I got this recipe right, I immediately made two more batches, ignored the moderation rule and ate way more than one person should. Je ne regrette rien.

Using an electric hand whisk beat together the margarine, sugars and vanilla in a mixing bowl, until light and fluffy. In another bowl, mix the flour, baking powder and salt. Sift flour mix into the margarine and stir until it is combined. *(If you use the electric beaters for this stage, the flour will fly everywhere.)* When the flour is safely combined, add the almond milk and then whisk until you have a smooth, sticky dough. Stir in the chocolate chips until they are evenly distributed.

Dollop the dough in dessertspoonfuls onto the baking sheet, keeping them well spaced apart. You should have 8 dollops per sheet. Smooth the tops a little with a clean finger until they are around 6cm across.

Bake for 14 minutes, turning the sheets halfway through to ensure they brown evenly. Allow to harden slightly on the tray for 2-3 minutes, then move to a wire rack to cool. If you are going to store them, wait until they are cold and store in an airtight container.

For a **ginger and chocolate chip variation**, add ½ tsp. of ground ginger with the flour. Substitute half of the chocolate chips with 75g of crystalised ginger, cut into small pieces.

Banana Bread

Makes one 1 1/2 lb. loaf

Prep - 5-10 minutes

Baking - 40 minutes

400g peeled ripe bananas

70g sunflower oil

90g light brown soft sugar

1 tsp vanilla extract

220g gluten-free self-raising flour

2 heaped tsp. baking powder

2 tbsp. sunflower seeds

Preheat the oven to 180°C. Line a 1 ½ lb loaf tin with non-stick greaseproof paper.

Banana Bread works at every meal and every need-for-a-nibble in between: a slice with a quickly snatched coffee for breakfast, a slice when it's not really lunchtime yet but your tummy is rumbling, a slice as a pick-me-up during an afternoon slump, a slice waiting for tea to cook, a slice with bananas and low-FODMAP custard for an easy pudding and a toasted slice with butter as a late night snack. During the holidays, the Young Master announced he was going to make lunch for the Little Miss and I. Thrilled there was one more meal I didn't have to make, I knew better than to complain when he presented three plates of toasted banana bread topped with a butter icing and some berries. The Little Miss could barely believe her luck!

This keeps well up to a week, wrapped in cling film or in an airtight container. You can double the mixture and freeze one, well wrapped in cling film and foil. I like this cake/bread because it creates minimal mess and is incredibly quick to make. For this reason, I have given you the weight of the oil needed as I simply put the bowl on the scales and pour the oil straight in.

Using a hand-held blender, puree the bananas in a medium-sized bowl. Add the oil, sugar and vanilla extract before quickly blending again.

Place a sieve on top of a larger mixing bowl. Place the bowl on top of your scales and set the scales to zero. Weigh the flour into the sieve and add the baking powder. Remove from the scales and sift the flour into the bowl. Make a well in the centre of the flour and pour the wet banana mixture into the well. Using a spatula, bring the batter together until it is thoroughly combined. Add the sunflower seeds and mix until they are evenly distributed.

Pour the batter into the tin and bake for 35-40 minutes until springy. Allow to cool for 5-10 minutes in the tin before removing to a wire rack to cool.

Chocolate Orange Sauce

Prep - 15-20 minutes

100g plain chocolate, broken into very small pieces

1 tbsp. golden syrup

20g butter

¼ tsp. orange oil

So many junk foods are out of bounds to us intolerant types. Yes, we'll have better skin, yes we're at less risk of coronary disease but some days I could just murder a bag of fun size Mars bars, or an entire chocolate orange. As important as it is to do the healthy, savoury stuff, it's just as important to have some emergency sweet rations up your sleeve to keep you on the Low-FODMAP wagon.

Chocolate Orange Sauce can be made ahead of time. I recommend you re-heat it by placing the jug into warm water to avoid ruining the sauce. Here I've made a plain, dark chocolate orange version but please substitute with a dairy-free 'milk' version if you prefer. If you can tolerate it, use 'normal' milk chocolate. Eat this with anything - sorbet, strawberries, pancakes, bananas, marshmallows, a large spoon...or as an impromptu chocolate fondue.

Place a heatproof bowl over a pan of gently simmering water on the hob ensuring a tight fit so no steam escapes into your sauce. The bowl should be lifted clear of the water. Place the chocolate in the bowl, just as it is around two-thirds melted and add the syrup, butter and orange extract.

Lightly stir once or twice with a wooden spoon then remove from the heat for it to continue melting. Please resist the temptation to stir too much as the chocolate will seize and it turn into a horrible, grainy, lumpy mess. It will melt in it's own time, be patient. As soon as all the chocolate is melted have a final gentle stir to combine the fat into the sauce. Pour into a warmed jug.

Variations on a Chocolatey Theme

Plain chocolate can take strong flavours – substitute the orange oil for any of the following, gently stirred through when the chocolate is melted: ½ tsp. salt flakes; ½ tsp. fresh, finely chopped red chilli; ½ tsp. freshly grated lime zest; ¼ tsp. freshly ground black pepper (long pepper for preference!); ¼ tsp. ground cinnamon; ½ tsp. vanilla extract; ½ tsp. finely grated fresh root ginger; 1 tsp. freeze-dried raspberries; 1 tsp. crème de cassis; 1 tsp. whisky; ½ tsp. instant espresso powder.

Rocky Road

Makes 64 squares

300g Plain chocolate, broken into small pieces

200g Plain biscuits crushed into crumbs

100g Mini-marshmallows

125g Coconut oil

3 tbsp. Golden syrup

You will need a 24cm square tin, lined with greaseproof paper.

Proceed with caution. This is GOOD, almost too good; it is impossible to eat just one piece. Try to ensure you have at some other people in the house, or you will eat it all. Of course you may be one of those people who has an enviable amount of self-control. Any extra can be frozen in a Tupperware container, it can defrost in five minutes. This is one of the few recipes that actually brings out the coconut flavour from the oil.

Check that the ingredients of your chocolate, biscuits and marshmallows are suitable for your dietary needs. Choose your preferred plain low-FODMAP biscuit or try using ginger flavoured biscuit and add 30g of finely chopped crystalised ginger. Similarly 20g of dried (not desiccated) coconut adds to the coconut flavour but if you are planning to eat the lot solo in one sitting (stranger things have happened), any more would be an unsafe amount of FODMAPs.

In a medium sized pan melt together the chocolate, syrup and coconut oil over a low heat gently stirring very occasionally. Be patient, chocolate doesn't like to be hurried. When it has all blended together take out a large ladleful and place in a warm bowl to keep it liquid.

Tip the biscuit crumbs, marshmallows and any other optional ingredients into the remaining mixture. Turn over the mixture using a large silicone spatula, until it is all coated. Press the mixture into the tin using the spatula until it is even, then pour over the reserved chocolate mix. Cover in cling film and chill in the fridge for a couple of hours until firm and set.

Lift out from the tin using the greaseproof paper then cut into squares (8 squares by 8 is my preferred size to work out!) Store in a greaseproof paper lined Tupperware with more paper between the layers. Keep in the fridge, as it is melts quite easily.

Nut and Seed Brittle (+ Variations)

Makes approx. 500g

Prep and cooking - 20 minutes

120g roasted salted peanuts

100g seed mix

50g light brown soft sugar

120 g white sugar

60g golden syrup

25g coconut oil

½ tsp. vanilla extract

½ tsp. bicarbonate of soda

You will need a sugar thermometer, 2 sheets greaseproof baking paper, at least 35cm wide, a clear work surface, and a rolling pin.

This recipe came about during a rare kitchen cupboard clear out – I had a lot of bags of seeds; each can't have had more than 10g in. It was such a successful experiment I now use ready mixed seed-mix of pumpkin, sunflower, sesame and linseeds. Use whatever ratio of seeds you prefer, or need to use up.

Prepare all your ingredients and work surface before you begin, as you will need to work very quickly once the sugar has started boiling.

Place the sugars and syrup in a heavy based pan over a medium heat. Swirl together as the sugar dissolves then stir in the coconut oil. When the oil is melted start bringing the sugar to the boil. Lay a sheet of greaseproof paper on a work surface. Using the sugar thermometer bring the sugar to 150C (or hard crack). Slide the pan off the heat.

Working quickly and using a wooden spoon, stir in the vanilla extract then the bicarbonate of soda, which will foam slightly. Finally add the nuts and seeds. Beat to mix well and carefully pour the mixture onto a greaseproof sheet. Spread slightly with the wooden spoon before covering with the second sheet of greaseproof paper. Use the rolling pin to quickly press the brittle into a shape about 8-10mm thick. Slide the greaseproof paper onto a cold baking sheet and allow to cool.

Once the brittle is cold, break into shards and pieces and store, layered with greaseproof paper in an airtight tin.

Variations

Once you have mastered the basic brittle, try any adding any combination of the following with the nuts:

With no vanilla - ½ tsp. of dried chilli flakes; ¼ tsp. freshly ground black pepper; ½ tsp. sweet smoked paprika

With vanilla - ¼ tsp. ground cinnamon.

Low-FODMAP Life Hacks

The way that I cope with the Low-FODMAP plan is to cook everything I can from scratch but this doesn't need to be the insurmountable task it feels! There are ways to save time and money on the Low-FODMAP diet and it's far easier to be organised when you're not feeling ill.

I *never* make one meal when there is the opportunity to make two or three. That's two or three day's worth of not cooking. Without my freezer I would have lost my mind many years ago.

Making your own seasonings may seem a bridge too far but kept in an airtight container, they will save you from a terminally bland and depressing diet. Some of the condiments I make are actually preferred by my non-low-FODMAP family.

Having homemade stock to hand saves you hours of reading labels and the frustration that EVERYTHING contains onion. It also comes under the banner of 'Nearly Free Food', which pleases me no end.

I have not had much success using the green parts of leeks or spring onions to replace onion flavouring but by jingo, we eat a lot of asafoetida. A jar will last a long time and replaces the specific onion hit essential for many recipes. Garlic oil is also a great saviour for that garlic-y hit without the oligos.

These Low-FODMAP life-hacks leave me more time to discover new and innovative ways to make my life more difficult.

Rice Porridge (+ 6 Variations)

Serves 1

Prep - 5 minutes + 15 minutes soaking.

Cooking - 5 minutes

125ml boiling water

125ml coconut milk, almond milk or a mixture of both

50g rice flakes

Pinch of salt - optional

Breakfast can be difficult in the winter months. Although there is cereal that my daughter can eat, I don't think it makes for the most balanced breakfast. Chia puddings seem popular but I can't cope with the fibre and I find the texture unpleasant so early in the morning.

Rice flakes make a good porridge. If you can leave the flakes and milk to stand for 15 minutes before cooking, the texture becomes smoother. This is co-incidentally the same amount of time it takes for me to shower – morning multitasking, right there. I use either almond milk, coconut milk or, more often, a mixture of both. The results are the same but the flavor is subtly different. Below is the recipe for one portion and our preferred serving suggestions.

In a small pan mix the milk and boiling water. Stir in the rice flakes and if you have the time, leave to soak for 15 minutes.

Over a medium heat, stir the porridge for 5 minutes. It will thicken considerably, once it is piping hot, remove to a bowl.

For a flavour that is full of **winter spices**, grate a little fresh nutmeg, ½ tsp. vanilla extract, pinch of cinnamon and 1 tsp. of soft brown sugar.

Toast some protein-packed **pumpkin seeds** and scatter over porridge that has been flavoured with a couple of drops of orange oil.

A tablespoon each of crushed **pecan nuts** and **maple syrup** will satisfy you until lunchtime.

Flavour the porridge with ½ tsp. of vanilla extract then **blueberries** will turn your porridge a lovely lilac as you stir in a small handful.

For high-days and holidays, push the boat out and add 15g of plain chocolate chips and a dash of orange oil. Yes, you read that correctly: I'm suggesting a **chocolate orange** for breakfast.

Try making the plain porridge in bulk and freezing in portion sizes. Remove from the freezer the night before and warm with your flavouring of choice in the morning. You may need a splash more water.

Beef Stock

Makes 1.5-2.5l

Prep 20 minutes

Cooking - 1 hour + 6-8 hours + 1 hour

250g beef bones, cut to a size that will fit in a large stockpot

250g carrots, washed and roughly chopped

160g tomatoes, cut into wedges

Very large handful of parsley stalks

3 bay leaves

6 large sage leaves

3-4 large sprigs of thyme

1 tbsp. black peppercorns

1 tsp. salt flakes

Preheat the oven to 200°C.

You will be looking at the cooking time for this recipe wondering if I've lost my mind – who in their right mind wants to cook for 9 ½ hours? Well dear reader, look at the prep time – that is not only very generous, but also spread across the 9 ½ hours.

Having your own Low-FODMAP, free-from beef stock feels such an achievement. The ingredients don't have to be too precise, I've given weights as stock doesn't mind wizened, misshapen or bendy veg. Please don't panic too much about getting the quantity of herbs right either, whatever amount you have to hand will be fine: just don't use rosemary as it can be overwhelming.

Place the bones in a large roasting tin with 500ml water and bake for 1 hour.

Place all the other ingredients in a large stockpot. Tip in the contents of the roasting tin, including any sticky bits. Cover with 4 litres of boiling water - you can use some of this boiling water to help scrape away any meat juices that have stuck on the tin. Bring to the boil, cover and turn down to a low simmer for up to 6-8 hours – the longer you can boil it the richer your stock will be.

Remove the large bones and strain the liquid through a sieve into a very large bowl (a bowl that can take 4 litres of water). Discard the bones, herbs and vegetables, rinse out the pan and return the stock to the pan.

If you have time, and I would urge you to make the time, put the stock to chill in a cold place – the fat will rise to the top and harden and be easier to remove. Keep any fat covered in the fridge to use when roasting potatoes.

You should have around 2.5 litres of stock. It is not vital that you boil the stock any further but I like to in order to maximise the rich flavour. Heat the stock uncovered, on a medium simmer for 1 hour until the stock has reduced to around 1.5 litres.

Once the stock has cooled, seal in either special freezer bags for liquids or in containers. I suggest you freeze in 500ml portions and unless you like to play a bit of freezer-lottery, I can't reiterate enough how important it is to label with the date contents and quantity.

Vegetable Stock

Makes 1.5l

Prep - 15 minutes

Cooking - 1 hour

260g peeled and chopped celeriac

175g peeled and chopped carrots

1 tbsp. olive oil

145g tomatoes, roughly chopped

1 tsp. black peppercorns

1 tsp. salt flakes

5 large parsley stalks

2 bay leaves

2 litres water

Possibly the most difficult aspect of the low-FODMAP diet is how to have an onion-free vegetable stock. As much as I love chicken and beef stock, I also love my vegetarian friends and they are just as welcome at our house for tea!

Celeriac can be a beast to peel but the rewards are worth it – as a rough guide an 850g globe, yields about 600g of peeled flesh. I certainly think this recipe is worth doubling; you are only limited by the size of your pan.

Heat the oil in a large pan over a high heat and add the celeriac and carrots. Cover and cook for 5 minutes, stirring often. Uncover and stir in the tomatoes, cooking for a further minute before stirring in all the rest of the ingredients.

Bring to the boil then turn down to a low simmer for an hour. Strain through a sieve and leave to cool. Store in 500ml portions in freezer safe containers.

As much as it pains my frugal self to say this – the leftover vegetables are tricky to re-purpose. Plucking out peppercorns is just too difficult!

Chicken Stock and Boiled Chicken

Makes 3.5 litres of light stock and 1.75 litres of rich stock

Prep - 10-15 minutes.

Cooking - Light stock and boiled chicken 1.5 hours

Rich stock - 2-3 hours

Light stock

2.5 kg chicken without giblets

160g carrots

2 bay leaves

1 tbsp. black peppercorns

Handful of parsley stalks

1 tsp. sea salt flakes

2 sage leaves

2 thyme sprigs

Rich Stock

Another quantity of carrots, bay leaves, black peppercorns, parsley stalks, sage, thyme and ½ tsp. sea salt flakes.

Possibly the most useful thing to have in the freezer – homemade low FODMAP, yeast-free, gluten-free, dairy-free chicken stock is a fast meal waiting to happen. The way I make my chicken stock really eeks out every last bit of chicken-y potential. I use the light stock in soups and stews and keep the rich stock for a sticky risotto or sauce. I keep thick parsley stalks, in the freezer for 'free' stock flavouring. The better the chicken, the better the stock – please use a free-range bird, high-welfare and locally grown if possible.

I use some the boiled chicken immediately for a chicken noodle soup and the rest is portioned up for a later meal. The dark meat doesn't mind being frozen in a well-sealed container and used for risotto. The light meat can be used in salads, pasta dishes, tacos and sandwiches either shredded by hand or sliced. The whole process doesn't need to be done in one go: the rich stock can be made later but please do take care that the chicken meat is not left lukewarm for hours – bacteria love lukewarm chicken.

Light Stock

Place the chicken in a large stockpot; remove any elastic or string tying it together. Add the remaining ingredients and cover with 4 litres of water.

Bring to the boil and reduce to a low simmer for 1.5 hours. Using tongs pull on the end of a leg – the chicken will be cooked when it easily pulls away. Allow to cool slightly, so you do not splash yourself with hot liquid and then remove the chicken to a large serving dish. I find it easiest to use a slotted spoon under the body of the chicken, as it will fall apart. Skim out any chicken pieces that have come away.

Cover the chicken with cling film to stop it drying out and allow it to cool. Strain the stock through a sieve into a very large bowl. Either discard the sieve-contents or put aside to go into the rich stock. Decant the light stock into containers or liquid safe freezer bags. I find it useful to measure 500ml, 250ml and 1 litre portions. Label with the date, contents and quantity.

Chicken Stock and Boiled Chicken

At this point I would keep 1.5 litres to make chicken noodle soup using the boiled chicken.

Rinse out the large pan and add the solids strained from the first boiling.

When the chicken is cool enough to handle remove the meat from the bones, separating the light and dark meat. Portion into containers and cool as quickly as possible.

Again, I would keep 400g of the light meat to make chicken noodle soup.

Dark Stock

Place the carcass and any remaining bits of chicken into the large pan with the new rich stock ingredients. Add 2 litres of water, cover and bring to the boil. Turn down to a low simmer for 2-3 hours. Strain the liquid through a sieve and portion into freezable containers.

Roasted Vegetables and their Uses

Makes 5 x 2 cup (approx. 400g) portions

Prep - 10 minutes

Baking - Up to 1 hour

4 tbsp. olive oil

6 peppers of different colours, 2 red, 2 yellow and 2 green for example, cut into 1" pieces

12 'salad' sized tomatoes quartered

2 courgettes, quartered lengthways then cut into 1cm slices.

4 tbsp. olive oil

2 large pinches of sea salt flakes and freshly ground black pepper.

Adjust the oven shelves to accommodate 2 large roasting tins. Preheat the oven to 200°C.

Technically baked, not roasted. When cooking in a hurry, roasted vegetables are one of the most useful things you can have in your freezer. This mixture is intended as a guide - the proportions can vary according to what you prefer or whatever there is a glut of! I try and use as many different coloured vegetables as possible. I keep these in vaguely 2 cup/ approximately 400g portions in the freezer to be pulled out for emergency vegetable situations, of which we seem to have a surprising amount. If you do have sensitivity to any of the vegetables, such as courgette, simply up the other vegetables. The baking time will depend on the ripeness of the vegetables – the sweeter they are, the quicker they will soften and cook.

Cut the courgettes in quarters lengthways then slice into 2cm pieces. Deseed the peppers and cut into roughly 2.5cm square pieces. Quarter the tomatoes

Put 2 tbsps. olive oil into each roasting tin. Split the vegetables evenly between the trays. Sprinkle a pinch of salt and about 8 grinds of pepper into each tray. Using your hands, turn the vegetables over in the oil.

Bake for 20 minutes then turn the vegetables over. Do be careful of the hot steam escaping when opening the oven. Repeat this every 20mins, for the next hour. If you are using in-season ripe vegetables you may find they have begun to char a little around the edges after only 30 minutes at which point you can remove them from the oven.

Empty the trays, vegetables, juices and all into a large bowl to cool. If you leave them in the trays, they will stick and will be really difficult to wash up. When completely cool, divide into suitable containers to freeze.

Now you've got your vitamins sorted, how should you use them?

I use the roasted vegetables for an **easy sauce bolognaise base** – brown 400g mince in a wide pan with a tablespoon of garlic oil. With a wand blender blitz together 1 portion of defrosted veg and a 400g can of tomatoes. Tip this into the browned mince, together with a tsp. of dried mixed Italian herbs and simmer together covered for 20 minutes until rich and thick. In the interests of timesaving, I would encourage you to double this mixture and freeze half.

Roasted Vegetables and their Uses

Concentrated tomatoes can be a trigger for some Type D IBS sufferers – if this is you, proceed with caution - For a **basic pasta sauce** - blitz together 1 can of chopped tomatoes, and a portion of roasted vegetables. If you happen to have fresh basil, add a handful of the leaves to the blitz-mix. Heat in a pan before stirring through the cooked pasta. Serve with lots of cheese atop and your children will not have a clue just how many vegetables they're eating.

As sauce for a **pizza base,** I use 500g passata, a portion of vegetables, ½ tsp. dried thyme, ½ dried oregano. Blitz together then heat through in a saucepan and reduce the liquid by around a quarter. I then use another portion of vegetables as a pizza topping; it's particularly lovely with goat's cheese.

A **quick taco filling** can be 300g chopped cooked chicken, warmed in a pan with a little olive oil, a portion of roasted vegetable and half a can of tomatoes. Cover the pan and heat through for 5 minutes, ensuring the chicken is heated all the way through. Job done. If you have no chicken, just use the vegetables and chopped tomatoes, and scattered toasted pumpkin seeds on top.

1 portion also works as a base for a **Cheese Scone Tatin**

A portion stirred through leftover pasta or boiled new potatoes with a protein of your choice makes for a good **packed lunch** dish.

Jazz up a **baked jacket potato** with a warm roasted vegetable topping.

The possibilities are endless and it is an easy way to eat a rainbow of vegetables.

Mild Curry Powder

Makes 4 heaped tablespoons

Prep - 10-15 minutes

Aside from the fact curry powder always tastes better when it is fresh, this is a useful tool to have in your Low-FODMAP toolkit, as commercially available powders all appear to contain garlic powder. Add more chilli to make it hotter or less if you're already hot enough...

2 tbsp. cumin seeds

2 ½ tbsp. coriander seeds

2tsp yellow mustard seed

2 tsp. turmeric

1 tsp. chilli flakes

1 tsp. ground ginger

½ tsp. asafoetida

½ tsp. salt flakes

Lightly toast the seeds in a hot, dry pan. When they start to pop, remove from the pan immediately. Using a pestle and mortar or spice grinder, add the remaining ingredients and grind to a powder.

Store in an airtight container, in a cool dark place.

Pesto

Prep - 5-10 minutes

Serves 8 (makes 300g)

5 large fistfuls fresh basil leaves, (approx. 120g)

2 tbsp. garlic oil

4 tbsp. olive oil

2 tbsp. fresh lemon juice

65g roughly chopped pecorino (or parmesan)

50g pine nuts

Freshly ground black pepper (about 6 good grinds)

Large pinch salt flakes

Eat half now and put half in the freezer. Try as a topping for a jacket potato or stirred into mashed potato, pasta or rice. Use as a dressing for a tomato salad. Stir pesto into leftover shredded chicken for a sandwich filling or mix with mayonnaise for a dip – I'm sure you know how to eat pesto!

Remove the tough stalks from the basil and place everything into a food processor, blitz until nearly smooth. Ta dah, it's done! This will keep refrigerated in a sealed container for up to a week. Ensure you keep the top covered with a thin film of olive oil. It will freeze in sealed container also covered in a thin film of oil for up to a month. This will need to defrost fully before eating – it does not microwave well.

Gooseberry Chutney

Makes 2 x 150ml jars

400g gooseberries

300ml non-brewed condiment

1 tsp. yellow mustard seeds

200g demerara sugar

½ tsp. asafoetida

1 tsp. salt

10g very finely chopped root ginger

Gooseberries fall into the very small range of 'Things-I-Can-Grow' – I need to treasure this very small achievement and turning a crop of homegrown gooseberries into a chutney is as good a way as any to keep the moment going.

In a heavy based pan, dry-fry the mustard seeds until they begin to pop then immediately remove them from the pan. Tip all the ingredients, including the now-toasted mustard seeds into the same heavy based pan and bring to the boil. Turn down to a low simmer for 45 minutes, stirring occasionally with a wooden spoon, until the berries have started to break up and the chutney is thickened. Spoon the chutney into warm, sterilised jars. Seal and clearly label.

The chutney improves with age; keep in a cool dark place for a couple of months. I like to keep mine until the autumn has begun to turn wintery and I need a reminder that once, it was warm, sunny and we could pick fruit.

Sweet and Sour Chilli Sauce

Serves 4 as a dipping sauce

Prep and cooking - 10 minutes

55ml non-brewed condiment

65g sugar

1 tbsp. tomato puree

1 tsp. dried chilli flakes

1 tbsp. cornflour

1 tbsp. fresh lime juice

40ml water

A handy little sauce to add fire to your belly; use with noodles or as a dipping sauce.

Whisk the cornflour and water together in a small bowl. Place all the remaining ingredients in a small pan and heat over a medium heat for 2 minutes until the sugar has dissolved. Remove from the heat, give the cornflour mix another quick whisk then whisk into the pan with the other ingredients. Return to the heat for 2 minutes, whisking continually as it thickens.

Decant to a suitable dipping dish or a warm, sterilised jar. Store unopened in the fridge for up to a month.

Flatbreads

By following the Pizza recipe for the pizza bases, you can quickly make lovely crisp flatbreads that are perfect for a meal with a Middle-Eastern vibe. Simply drizzle the bases with olive oil, flavoured or plain, then scatter over either crunchy salt flakes, freshly ground black pepper, herbed grey salt, za'atar, sweet smoked paprika or chilli flakes.

Bake for 8-10 minutes. These breads are best when broken with friends and used to scoop up all sorts of dips and salsas.

Tomato Barbeque Sauce

Prep - 5 minutes

Cooking - 15 minutes.

Makes 350ml

1 x tbsp. garlic oil

2 x tsp. sweet smoked paprika

½ tsp. sea salt flakes

350ml passata or sieved tomatoes

2 tbsp. dark muscovado sugar

2 tsp. maple syrup

2 tsp. lemon juice

¼ tsp. hickory liquid smoke

You will need a sterilized, warmed jar to store the sauce.

Some foods require a bit of moisture on the side to be dipped into. So many ketchups and commercially sold sauces contain garlic and onion, it can be a minefield when all you want is something to go on the end of a chip or chicken nugget. I know, I'm classy like that. For a livelier sauce, add ½ tsp. of dried chilli flakes with the rest of the spices. Delicious atop any taco, particularly one with pulled pork or chicken.

Fructose malabsorbtion can cause issues for some IBS sufferers – tomatoes, being a fruit, if concentrated, cause such issues. However, this is a condiment and unless gluttony gets the better of you, 2 tablespoons of sieved tomatoes are generally tolerated by most on the Low-FODMAP diet. If you can't lay your hands on liquid smoke, it's not the end of the world, you will still have a delicious sauce.

Warm the oil in a medium sized pan over a medium high heat. Add the paprika and stir until the paprika is releasing its warm aroma. Pour in the rest of the ingredients and bring to a low simmer for 15 minutes, stirring occasionally.

Pour into the sterilized jar and seal. This will keep unopened in the fridge for a month but once opened keep refrigerated and use within a fortnight.

Cranberry Sauce

Prep - 5 minutes

Cooking - 10 minutes

250g cranberries

120ml water

Juice of 2 oranges

Finely shredded zest of ½ orange

150g caster sugar

10 allspice berries

If you are not eating this straight away, ensure you have a warm sterilised jar on standby

Cranberry sauce is now readily available in a Low-FODMAP friendly version but I find all the versions a bit dull. Yes they taste of cranberries but that's about it. I like my cranberry sauce to have a little more oomph about it. My children aren't big fans of roast dinners but a serving of cranberry sauce on the side distracts them. It is also useful if you are not entirely convinced your meal is going to be well received – a dollop of cranberry sauce and your diners forget to put up a protest.

Ideally you will have reserved the cranberries that you have been flavouring vodka with but it's not essential. I have found there is little difference between using fresh or frozen cranberries. You will need a warmed sterilised preferably flip top jar to store this in. Unopened it will keep for several months in a cool dark place. Once opened, store in the fridge.

Place all the ingredients in a medium pan and bring to a simmer, uncovered over a medium high heat for 10 minutes, stirring with a wooden spoon. The cranberries will have started to burst, remove from the heat and beat with the wooden spoon to encourage even more bursting. Return to the heat for another minute before decanting into your jar or bowl.

Flavouring Vodka and Gin

Flip-top bottles

Labels

A funnel

A muslin square

A large tightly lidded glass jar for the steeping phase. If you are steeping larger items it is so much easier to get them out of a jar than through a tiny bottleneck.

I give all the jars and bottles a good wash which helps warm the glass before pouring boiling water over and in them to sterilise.

People are often stunned when I say I don't drink wine or beer. So what DO you drink? Vodka and gin I say. Which again brings an outpouring of grief on my behalf. I'm not sorry; I remember the days of having to leave a night-out early because of stomachache or such severe yeasty bloating that I couldn't bend in my, now excruciatingly tight, clothes. I used to love drinking wine but once I realised it was one of things making me feel so ill, it really was not that much of a chore to avoid it completely.

That's not to say I don't appreciate variety. Vodka/gin tonic is only so interesting; I like to spice things up my own way. It's astonishingly easy to flavour spirits. Over the years I've had a higher number of hits than misses. Pre-low FODMAP I made darned good lychee vodka or an autumnal apple and cinnamon but here I'll share with you my current favourites. Many people like to flavour their vodkas with whole sweets or toffees. I'm not keen, I don't really like a syrupy flavour but if that's your bag, try it!

Generally I'll drink them with a soda or tonic mixer and ice. Lime accompanies most of these flavours well but the fun starts when you start mixing the vodkas - Cranberry and Ginger Collins? Yes please! I use them in cooking to replace a splash of wine, this way I can add my own customised flavour to a dish.

Cranberry Vodka – the daintiest of pinks

Wash 150g fresh or frozen cranberries. Prick each berry a couple of times with something sharp like a cocktail stick. Place the cranberries in the large sterilised jar and pour over 750ml of vodka. Give it a little shake, and then shake twice daily for the next week. Strain through a scalded muslin into sterilised bottles, label and seal. Retain these cranberries and use for a cranberry sauce with a bit of welly.

Ginger Vodka

Take a good bulb of fresh root ginger. Wash and peel then slice into wide strips. Place the ginger in the sterilised jar, cover with 750ml of vodka. Give it a shake, then shake twice daily for the next week, fortnight or month, depending on how fiery you like your ginger. Strain through a scalded muslin into sterilised bottles, seal and label.

Flavouring Vodka and Gin

Vanilla Vodka

Anyone who thinks vanilla is bland has been tasting the wrong vanilla; it's a musky, sexy, complex flavour. Split a vanilla pod lengthways and put straight into a 500ml bottle of vodka. It will be ready in a week but I like to leave the pod where it is. Add it to rhubarb vodka and you have rhubarb and custard in a shot glass. It also works with coke for a taste like a coke float.

Hot Chilli Vodka

This will turn your Bloody Marys up to 11. I also use this quite a lot in cooking for a final kick when I don't really want a whole chilli in there. I am not going to give you a chilli quantity, have a think about how hot you really like things. I don't like things so hot that my ears hurt, so I use 4 small red chillies per litre of vodka. If you can take scotch bonnets or birds eye chillies then be my guest! Wash and dry the whole chillies, then prick each chilli several times. Place in a large sterilized glass jar and cover with 750ml vodka. Shake the jar then shake twice daily for the next 5 days. Strain through a scalded muslin into sterilised bottles, seal and label.

Orange Gin

This really is the most delicious way to enjoy a gin and tonic. It has the orangey punch of Cointreau but without the syrupy flavour. I cannot recommend this highly enough as Christmas presents. The gin does not necessarily need to be artisanal or expensive as you are adding more than enough flavour. One that doesn't taste of paint-stripper is a good guide. Scrub 3 oranges and peel them using a vegetable peeler. This is the most efficient way of removing the lovely zest without adding the bitter pith. Place in your sterilised jar, cover with a litre of vodka and shake once a day. This can sit for up to 6 months this way, but 3 weeks will suffice. Strain through a scalded muslin into sterilised bottles, label and seal. For a naughty St. Clements, mix orange gin in equal parts with limoncello, strain over ice and serve in a martini glass.

Flavouring Vodka and Gin

Cucumber Vodka

Come summertime I miss Pimms. My salvation has been cucumber vodka served with a sparkling elderflower mixer over ice with lime and cucumber slices. Take 1 short cucumber, preferably organic, peel and slice into thick wedges. Place in your sterilised jar and pour over 750ml of vodka. Lightly agitate so as not to break up the wedges then do so twice daily for the next week. It will take on the most delicate shade of *eau de nil*. Strain through a scalded muslin into sterilised bottles, seal and label. *Unless you have to drive somewhere later, try one of the discarded cucumbers, they're curiously moreish.*

Christmas Spiced Vodka

A cautious hand is needed here to avoid the drink tasting like something from the dentist. Take the peel from 2 washed and scrubbed clementines, 1 stick of cinnamon, 1 whole star anise, 4 allspice berries and, as an exception to my flavouring rule, a tablespoon of soft brown sugar. Place in your sterilised jar and cover with a litre of vodka. Let it sit for a fortnight with twice daily agitation (the vodka, not you), strain through scalded muslin into sterilised bottles, seal and label.

Raspberry Vodka

Raspberries and lemon marry beautifully so good quality lemonade is all the mixer this needs. I give this a vigorous shake, as I want to get as much raspberry juice into the vodka as possible. By the end of the week, the raspberries will have lost most of their colour. Wash 150g of raspberries and leave to drain dry. Place the raspberries in the large sterilised jar and pour over 750ml of vodka. Give it a little shake, and then shake twice daily for the next week. Strain through a scalded muslin into sterilised bottles, label and seal.

Index

Index

Index

Acknowledgements

Thank you to everyone that has held my hand throughout this project and taught me it is easier to walk one step at a time, even with a dodgy ankle. The Bobcat Crew, Frenchie and Yale Laydeez, have endured more than their fair share, for which I am eternally grateful. Heartfelt thanks to Anthony Twist RD for making the Little Miss and me feel our happy selves. For every person that has fed me coffee, cared for my children, embraced the gin owl, given me a lift, unpicked a semi-coherent rambling, eaten my kitchen disasters (and been brave enough to try again), patiently explained the intricacies of the internet, fonts or publishing - I am indebted, thank you.

Carla, thank you for patiently translating my inklings and feelings into a thing, a real life thing!

My parents and family have been a continuous support, a very big thank you. Mum, thank you for your years of effort in trying to solve a problem like Laura's tummy, with no help from Hilda Reader.

My darling Nippers - you have been so patient and encouraging, while your house has been turned upside down and Mummy just needed '5 minutes more'. I have listened to your appraisals of every recipe and I hope you agree these are the right 'one for the book'? I love you entirely.

Finally Richard. Thank you for everything, Thisledome.

Do pop into Our House For Tea, www.ourhousefortea.com, for further adventures in Low-FODMAP and Free-From Cookery. Contact us - contact@ourhousefortea.com

Copyright ©Laura Stonehouse 2016. All rights reserved.

All photography, ©Richard Stonehouse, Stonehouse Photographic, www.stonehousephotographic.com

Layout, Carla Boulton, www.carlaboulton.co.uk

First published in 2016 by Pebbleshed Publishing

ISBN: 978-0-9957663-0-3

Lightning Source UK Ltd.
Milton Keynes UK
UKOW07f1354291016
286388UK00002B/14/P